FORGERS

Lance Salway

FORGERS

KESTREL BOOKS

KESTREL BOOKS
Published by Penguin Books Ltd
Harmondsworth, Middlesex, England

Copyright © 1979 by Lance Salway

All rights reserved. No part of this publication may be reproduced, stored in a retrieval system, or transmitted in any form or by any means, electronic, mechanical, photocopying, recording, or otherwise, without the prior permission of the Copyright owner.

First Published 1979

ISBN 0 7226 5469 3

Printed in Great Britain by
Fakenham Press Limited
Fakenham, Norfolk

For Sara, Rachel and Diana

Contents

1	Ten Million Dollars!	9
2	Fairground Fakes	10
3	The Great Barnum	15
4	Creatures Great and Small	21
5	Counterfeit Kings . . .	25
6	. . . and Perfect Gentlemen	32
7	'Mincemeat swallowed whole'	39
8	The Piltdown Man	44
9	Flint Jack	49
10	The Marvellous Boy	55
11	The Boy Who Wrote a Play by Shakespeare	61
12	The Master Forger	67
13	'King' David and the Yorkshire Coiners	73
14	The Greatest Forgery of All	80
15	The Hungarian Circle	85
16	Forging Ahead!	89
	Further Reading	91
	Acknowledgements	93
	Index	94

1 · Ten Million Dollars!

Pagham is a quiet village near Chichester in Sussex. It was here, one evening in April 1977, that officers of the Scotland Yard Currency Squad, the Special Crimes Squad and Sussex police smashed what is believed to have been the biggest counterfeiting operation ever organized in Britain.

Detectives had been trying for months to locate the source of thousands of forged American dollar bills which had been turning up all over Europe during the tourist season. Their investigations had led them to a bungalow in Pagham. There, behind a false wall in the garage, they found a secret room containing photographic equipment, printing presses, paper and ink. They also discovered a large quantity of forged fifty and twenty dollar bills, all packed and ready for distribution. The total value of the notes they found came to ten million dollars. Scotland Yard were delighted with the success of the raid. The officer in charge of the operation claimed that 'this must rate as one of the most significant captures in this field in recent times'.

Most people tend to imagine forgers as being dedicated criminals like those who made the dollar bills at Pagham. But there is more to forgery than counterfeit banknotes – it extends into all branches of art and archaeology, literature and science. And the forgers themselves are often just as fascinating as their fakes. Some, like Han van Meegeren and Flint Jack, have been gifted artists who resorted to forgery in order to fool the experts or to gain recognition for their own work. Others, like the Yorkshire coiners and the Hungarian Circle, have been hardened criminals. But the most successful forgers of all have been those whose identities were never discovered.

Here are some of their stories.

2 · Fairground Fakes

Forgers thrive on human gullibility. Their frauds and fakes succeed only because people *want* to believe that what they see is real. Throughout history people have exploited this human weakness but few deceptions have been more outrageous than those of the travelling showmen of the nineteenth century.

In the days before films, radio and television transformed the lives of ordinary people, one of the principal sources of entertainment was the travelling fair. Unlike fairs today, which consist mainly of roundabouts, dodgem cars and similar amusements, a large proportion of these early fairs was composed of stalls which exhibited human and animal freaks. The sideshows were operated by showmen whose sole intention was to persuade the public to part with their money in order to set eyes on fat men, giant women, living skeletons, two-headed ladies and other bizarre attractions. Many of these exhibits were genuine for the travelling fair was often the only refuge for people whose appearance was unusual or deformed. But most of the sideshow freaks were forgeries. Ordinary country people had a very limited knowledge of the world and they were quite prepared to believe that fortune-telling ponies, spotted Hottentots and giant snakes really did exist and could be seen in their village on payment of a penny.

One of the most famous sideshow attractions of the time was Madame Stevens, 'the pig-faced lady'. Madame Stevens was really a bear whose face and paws had been shaved. She was strapped into a chair and dressed in women's clothes which, because of the fashions of the time, made her look convincingly human. A table was placed in front of her, under which was hidden a boy armed with a stick. 'Lord' George Sanger, himself a distinguished showman, has left us a record of the proprietor's patter:

'I call your attention, ladies and gentlemen, to the greatest wonder of the world! Behold and marvel! Madame Stevens, the pig-faced lady, who is now in her eighteenth year. I believe that is correct, miss?' (Here the hidden boy would prod the bear, who gave a grunt.) 'As you see, ladies and gentlemen, the young lady understands what is said perfectly, though the peculiar formation of her jaws has deprived her of the power of uttering human speech in return.

Forgers

'You were born at Preston in Lancashire?' (Another prod and another grunt.) 'Quite so. And you enjoy good health and are very happy?' (Another prod and grunt.) 'You are inclined, I suppose, as other ladies, to be led by some gentleman into the holy bonds of matrimony?' (Here the boy would give an extra prod, causing the bear to grunt angrily.) 'What, no! Well, well, don't be cross because I asked you!'

This would be sure to raise a laugh and expressions of wonder. Then a plate would be passed round to receive contributions 'to buy the lady small comforts and luxuries', as the showman said.

Not all sideshow attractions were as bizarre or as cruel as this one. Most deceptions were harmless enough. Madame Gomez, the tallest woman in the world, was really only six feet tall but stood on a seven inch high platform that was easily concealed under her long dress. Tamee Ahmee and Orio Rio, 'the savage cannibal pygmies', were two children cleverly disguised with make-up, feathers and beads.

Some of Barnum's exhibits at Olympia in 1889

Fairground Fakes

In the early days of his career, the showman David Prince Miller once played the part of a black giantess when that lady suddenly left a fair to get married. Here is his own account of what happened:

> I consequently was attired in a fantastic sort of dress, which was composed of feathers, beads, etc., and was exhibited as the great black giantess, nearly eight feet high; of course, my face had to undergo the operation of being blackened with burned cork and grease.
>
> As a matter of course, I was totally unacquainted with the English language, and had only been in this country a few weeks; that I was brought over by Captain Somebody, at tremendous expense, and only permitted to be exhibited for a limited period, previous to my return to my own country. A conversation was held between me and my proprietor, in a language which neither of us could understand, nor anyone else comprehend, but which he interpreted to the audience.
>
> We had a very good fair, but some of our visitors expressed their doubts as to my being what was alleged. Sometimes a drunken fellow would attempt to take liberties with me, when my outraged delicacy would most indignantly repel the insult by giving the fellow a sound thump on the head; indeed I was compelled to be very violent, for too close an inspection would have exposed the whole affair. One day a sturdy fellow seemed resolved to have a kiss, I resisted with all my might, but was overpowered; the gentleman not only got a kiss, but a face nearly as black as my own, a considerable quantity of my complexion being transferred from my face to his, presenting to the lookers-on a rather ludicrous appearance. We should have done very well to have exhibited as the piebald twins, his face and mine being half black and half white. The crowd retired from the caravan, expressing their contempt at the exhibition; but amidst the noisy din of drums and trumpets, nobody heard them – the proprietor at the same time bawling through a speaking trumpet, 'Hear what they say of the black giantess, never saw such a sight before; hear them – they say it's worth a shilling a piece! Come on, only a penny!' and another crowd would rush in to see the gigantic black Indian queen, as I was denominated.
>
> I soon became tired of the confinement necessary to this engagement, and gave up the situation.

It is hardly surprising that the public should have been sceptical of Miller's impersonation. Even by the standards of a travelling country fair, it was a very feeble fraud indeed.

Forgers

While David Prince Miller was learning his trade in small English fairs, the greatest showman of them all was busy duping the public on the other side of the Atlantic. But Phineas Taylor Barnum was not content with pig-faced ladies or black giantesses – his fairground fakes were to be the most spectacular of all.

3 · *The Great Barnum*

In 1834 a penniless young man called Phineas Taylor Barnum arrived in New York with his family, determined to make a fortune. He had been born in the small town of Bethel in Connecticut, and it was there that he had started his career as one of the most spectacular hoaxers of all time. He had worked for a while in a barter store – a shop where goods were traded for items brought in by the customers – and he swindled his way to success. The customers did their best to cheat Barnum but he was able to beat them at their own game: coffee was made of burned peas, cotton was labelled wool and, in Barnum's own words, 'everything was different from what it represented'. He learned early in life that 'there's a sucker born every minute' and, when he died in 1890, he left a fortune of five million dollars to prove it.

Barnum started his career as a showman in style. In 1835 a friend told him about an extraordinary old woman who was being exhibited in Philadelphia. Her name was Joice Heth and not only was she supposed to be 161 years old but she also claimed to have been the nurse to George Washington, the first president of the United States. Barnum at once went to inspect the phenomenon. He found a hideous crone lying on a couch. Her legs were paralysed and she was toothless and blind. She was a cheerful soul, though, and told Barnum about her time as nurse to 'dear little George' and showed him the bill of sale for 'one negro woman, named Joice Heth, aged fifty-four years'. It was dated 1727 and was signed by Washington's father. Barnum was impressed by this evidence – or so he later claimed. He immediately borrowed money to buy Joice Heth from her proprietor to exhibit her himself in New York. This was the opportunity he had been waiting for.

From the beginning, the secret of Barnum's extraordinary success stemmed not so much from his exhibits as from his skilful use of publicity. He was the first showman to appreciate that any kind of publicity is better than none and that it doesn't matter what people say about you as long as they mention your name. Posters and advertisements announcing the exhibition of Joice Heth were soon plastered all over New York:

> The greatest curiosity in the world, and the most interesting, particularly to Americans, is now exhibiting at the Saloon fronting on Broadway, JOICE HETH, nurse to General George Washington (the father of our country), who has arrived at the astonishing age of 161 years, as authentic documents will prove, and in full possession of her mental faculties. She is cheerful and healthy, although she weighs but forty-nine pounds. She relates many anecdotes of her young master; she speaks also of the red-coats during the Revolutionary War, but does not appear to hold them in high estimation ...
>
> She has been a member of the Baptist Church for upwards of one hundred years, and seems to take great satisfaction in the conversation of ministers who visit her. She frequently sings and repeats parts of hymns and psalms.

New York flocked to see Joice Heth, and the press, then as now eager for a good story, sang her praises. 'Her appearance is much like an Egyptian mummy just escaped from its sarcophagus,' wrote the *New York Evening Star*, adding that the lady had told their reporter that she had been smoking a pipe for 120 years. The

The Great Barnum

Daily Advertiser claimed that 'ancient or modern times furnish no parallel to the great age of this woman'.

Barnum later took Joice Heth to Boston where her success was repeated. When interest there began to die down, a letter appeared in a local newspaper which claimed that Joice Heth was a fraud. 'What purports to be a remarkable old woman,' wrote the anonymous correspondent, 'is simply a curiously constructed automaton, made of whalebone, india-rubber, and numberless springs ingeniously put together, and made to move at the slightest touch, according to the will of the operator. The exhibitor is a ventriloquist, and all the conversations apparently held with the ancient lady are purely imaginary.' The writer of the letter was, of course, Barnum himself. He knew that controversy was the best publicity, and business picked up splendidly for the rest of his stay in Boston.

And then, in 1836, Joice Heth died. Barnum arranged for a distinguished New York surgeon to dissect the body before a large gathering of witnesses. The results of the post-mortem showed that Joice Heth could not have been more than eighty years old when she died! Barnum was immediately accused of duping the press and public but he protested that he had hired Joice Heth in all good faith. It seems hard to believe that an astute man like Barnum could really have believed that Joice Heth was 161 years old but, whatever the truth of his part in the deception, the uproar did his reputation no harm at all.

In 1841 Barnum opened the American Museum in New York as a permanent exhibition of natural history, art and curiosities. The exhibits were not limited to freaks – they included live and stuffed animals, paintings, and a remarkable working model of the Niagara Falls. Entertainments of different kinds took place there too, including the first Punch and Judy show ever to be seen in the United States. Within a year Barnum made the American Museum the most popular place of entertainment in the country. 'I meant to make people talk about my Museum,' he said later, 'to exclaim over its wonders; to have men and women all over the country say: "There is no place in the United States where so much can be seen for twenty-five cents as in Barnum's American Museum."' To do this, he diligently sought out bizarre attractions to lure the public, presenting them at various times with

grizzly bears, giant snakes, fat boys, dwarfs, rope dancers and Red Indians. His skill with words made the exhibits seem even more wonderful than they were: a hippopotamus was advertised

The Great Barnum

as 'The Great Behemoth of the Scriptures' and his performing fleas were 'harnessed to carriages and other vehicles of several times their own weight, which they will draw with as much precision as a cart-horse'.

In 1842 Barnum exhibited one of his most famous forgeries: the Feejee Mermaid. Early that year a Boston showman called on Barnum and showed him a strange, repulsive creature which, he claimed, was a mermaid. Even Barnum had to admit that it was 'an ugly, dried-up, black-looking, and diminutive specimen', but he asked a naturalist to examine it to see whether or not it was genuine. The expert was puzzled by the creature because he found that the spine continued in an unbroken line from the tail to the base of the skull. He confessed to Barnum that he had no idea how the mermaid could have been manufactured.

'Then why do you suppose it is manufactured?' Barnum asked him.

'Because I don't believe in mermaids,' the naturalist replied.

'That is no reason at all,' said Barnum, 'and therefore *I'll* believe in the mermaid, and hire it.'

Barnum had persuaded himself that the mermaid was real. All he had to do now was persuade the public too. He kept his new acquisition secret for the time being while he distributed ten thousand copies of a leaflet which set out to prove that mermaids really did exist. It was illustrated with engravings which showed them lying on rocks and combing their hair. Barnum's name was not mentioned and neither was his hideous new exhibit.

Then, having awakened public interest in mermaids, Barnum announced the arrival of his own specimen. People flocked to see it. There were some ugly scenes when it was discovered that the Feejee Mermaid was not the beautiful creature that people had expected. But, on the whole, the public seemed satisfied, and Barnum laughed all the way to the bank. The mermaid was, of course, a fake. It had been made years before by a Japanese fisherman who had joined the upper half of a monkey to the lower half of a fish.

The Feejee Mermaid did not impress all the visitors who came to see it. One of them said to Barnum, 'I lived two years on the Fiji Islands, and I never heard of any such thing as a mermaid.'

Barnum's reply was characteristic. 'There's no accounting for some men's ignorance,' he said.

Like all showmen, Barnum set out to exploit this ignorance. He is supposed to have said that 'you can fool all the people some of the time, and some of the people all of the time, but you cannot fool all the people all of the time'. Barnum, the prince of hoaxers, managed to fool more people than most.

A griffin

4 · Creatures Great and Small

Barnum's Feejee Mermaid was neither the first fake mermaid ever made nor was it the first mythical creature to be exhibited for the entertainment of the public. From earliest times people have been fascinated by monsters and extraordinary animals, and it was inevitable that forgers should exploit this basic human curiosity.

Ancient mythology is rich in bizarre creatures. The griffin was an animal with the body of a lion and the head and wings of an eagle. The chimera was reputed to have the head of a lion, the body of a she-goat and the hind-quarters of a dragon. The more harmless centaur combined the upper half of a human being with the legs and body of a horse. Stories of creatures such as these were absorbed into the literature and mythology of later generations too, so that people in the Middle Ages were quite content to believe in the possible existence of sea serpents, mermaids and the many-headed hydra. We may laugh today at such gullibility and congratulate ourselves on our superior knowledge of the animal world. And yet, even now, some of us are convinced that the Abominable Snowman exists in the Himalayas and that a monstrous serpent is living under the calm waters of Loch Ness. Perhaps we are not as sophisticated as we like to think.

Forgers

Of all the mythical monsters, the basilisk or cockatrice was supposed to be the most fearsome and bizarre. It was said to be a kind of hideous small dragon which came from an egg laid by a seven-year-old cock bird. The egg was round, had no shell and could only be hatched by a toad. The monster was so ugly that it would die of fright if it saw itself in a mirror. It is little wonder that this charming creature should intrigue forgers of animals. No one had ever seen a live basilisk and so no one could tell what a dead one looked like. It was therefore comparatively easy to fake.

A basilisk

The method was simple and ingenious and has varied little from earliest times to our own. G. P. Whitley gave a convenient recipe for making a basilisk – or a jenny haniver, as they are now called for no known reason – in the *Australian Magazine* in 1928. First, take a small skate,

curling its side fins over its back, and twisting its tail into any required position. A piece of string is tied round the head behind the jaws to form a neck and the skate is dried in the sun. During the subsequent shrinkage, the jaws project to form a snout and a hitherto concealed arch of cartilage protrudes so as to resemble folded arms. The nostrils, situated a little above the jaws, are transformed into a quaint pair of eyes, the olfactory laminae resembling eye-lashes. The result of this simple process, preserved with a coat of varnish and perhaps ornamented with a few dabs of paint, is a jenny haniver, well calculated to excite wonder in anyone interested in marine curios.

It is not known when jenny hanivers were first made, but pictures of them can be found in sixteenth-century books and they have certainly been produced ever since. Tourists can buy them in Mexico, and they are even found in London from time to time.

A jenny haniver

Fake sea serpents and monsters have always been popular too, and even today we still hear occasional reports of mysterious monstrous fish being washed ashore in different parts of the world. On examination, though, most of these turn out to be distorted sharks or whales. The most ambitious fake sea serpent was exhibited in New York by Dr Albert Koch in 1845. It consisted of the skeleton of an enormous sea serpent thirty-five metres long, including a head and ribs. The public flocked to see it but it was unfortunate for Dr Koch that one of the visitors was a professor of anatomy who announced that the skull was that of a mammal and that the bones had come from several different skeletons, mainly those of whales.

Recent animal fakes tend to be hoaxes rather than deliberate attempts to deceive or defraud the public. The City Museum of Wakefield, Yorkshire, possesses a fine specimen of the Noctifer, a skilful combination of a bittern and an eagle-owl. On display at the Royal Scottish Museum in Edinburgh are the Gruck, a bird consisting of the head of a duck and the body of a grouse, and the Bare-fronted Hoodwink, an elegant fowl composed of the head of a crow, the body of a plover and the wings and tail feathers of a

Noctifer   *White Russian Shore-Muddler*

duck. This museum also possesses the only known specimen of the very rare Fur-bearing Trout which, according to the label, grows a dense coat of white fur to protect it from the cold water in which it lives. This fish was presented to the museum by a lady who had bought it in Canada under the firm belief that it was genuine. A particularly ingenious fake was made in Sweden at the Göteborg Museum in a deliberate attempt to attract visitors. The White Russian Shore-Muddler is exhibited once a year on April Fool's Day. It consists of the head and foreparts of a baby wild pig, the teeth of an alligator, and the hind-quarters and tail of a squirrel. The back feet are those of a water fowl.

We are rarely deceived now by animal fakes. But we can still laugh at them, and it would seem that forgers of animals do, on the whole, have a sense of humour. Forgers in other fields, though, are rarely interested in making people laugh. Forgery can be a serious business, sometimes even a matter of life or death.

5 · Counterfeit Kings ...

There are many different kinds of fake, but it is perhaps the human variety which requires the greatest amount of cunning and bravado. The forger of banknotes and pictures or mermaids and manuscripts must possess a high degree of technical ingenuity but the task of the human fraud is even more demanding. It is not enough for an impostor merely to *look* like the person he or she is trying to impersonate; he must also possess a detailed knowledge of the life and behaviour of his subject, and have the skill, confidence and determination to convince the world that he really is someone else.

There are many reasons why people try to impersonate others. Some do it for money and position, or to make fools of the public at large. Some do it just for fun. Others, like those who pretend to be kings or princesses, may well be driven by political ambition or by a desire for power. These royal fakes are often the victims of unscrupulous people who exploit the particular skills of the impersonator for their own ends.

Royal fakes have appeared from time to time throughout history. One of the earliest cases was that of Terentius Maximus who, in the year 73, claimed to be the Emperor Nero. In the nineteenth century, at least thirty people pretended at different times to be the son of King Louis XVI of France, who was supposed to have died during the French Revolution. England, too, has had its share of royal impostors, though few have been as convincing or as courageous as Lambert Simnel and Perkin Warbeck.

When Richard III was killed at the Battle of Bosworth in 1485, he left no direct heir to the throne. His only son had died the year before and the Plantagenet heir was now his nephew, the ten-year-old Earl of Warwick. The new king, Henry VII, was well aware that the young Earl had more right to the throne than he had himself, and he realized, too, that as long as the boy remained free his crown would not be secure. The solution was simple: Warwick was imprisoned in the Tower of London where he was to remain for the rest of his life. But, even in the Tower, Warwick posed a threat to the new king. Many people refused to believe that he really *was* a prisoner, and there was even talk that the boy king Edward V and his brother – 'the princes in the Tower' – were still alive. These princes, the sons of King Edward IV, had been placed under the protection of their uncle, later Richard III, when their father died. They were taken to the Tower of London for safety and it was there that they were mysteriously murdered. It is thought that their deaths had been ordered by Richard so that he could inherit the throne himself but others have suggested that Henry VII was responsible.

It is hardly surprising that impostors should have taken advantage of these rumours. The first of these was a young man called Lambert Simnel who was about the same age as the Earl of Warwick. He was the son of a tradesman, and was described at the time as being 'not only beautiful and graceful in person, but witty and ingenious'. An ambitious priest called Richard Simons met Simnel and decided to pass him off as the young Earl of Warwick, the rightful king of England. Simons took Simnel to Ireland, where Richard III had always been popular, and announced that Warwick had escaped from the Tower. Simnel's personality and story were so convincing that he was crowned by the Bishop of Meath as King Edward VI on 24 May 1487.

Simnel's supporters then decided to try their luck in England. With the help of the Duchess of Burgundy, a sister of Richard III, Simnel assembled a small force of some fifteen hundred German mercenaries and sailed for England. He landed on the Lancashire coast in June 1487 but his progress south was halted by the king's army at Stoke-on-Trent where, after a long, hard battle, Simnel was defeated and taken prisoner.

Henry had been more amused than worried by Simnel's claim to be the rightful king. After all, he only needed to remove the real Earl of Warwick from his prison and show him to the people in order to prove that Simnel was a fake. The king did this, and then displayed his contempt for the pretender by sentencing him not to death but to service in the royal kitchen as a scullion. Lambert Simnel's royal adventure was over.

Forgers

Four years later, Perkin Warbeck posed a far more serious threat to Henry's security. The new pretender was born in Flanders in about 1475 and was far superior to Lambert Simnel in education, intellect and social position. Like Simnel, he too began his campaign in Ireland where he announced that he was Richard, Duke of York, the younger of the two princes supposed to have been murdered in the Tower. He raised support for his cause there and then returned to Flanders where, like Simnel before him, he convinced the Duchess of Burgundy that he was the rightful king. With the assistance of the Emperor of Austria, they prepared to invade England. The invasion failed miserably and Warbeck was forced to retreat to Scotland, where he acquired the support of James IV and married a Scottish noblewoman. He was now openly claiming to be King Richard IV of England and Henry realized that the new pretender had to be taken very seriously indeed. Warbeck then moved to Cornwall to take advantage of local unrest against taxation and received a warm welcome. In 1497 he raised an army and marched towards London.

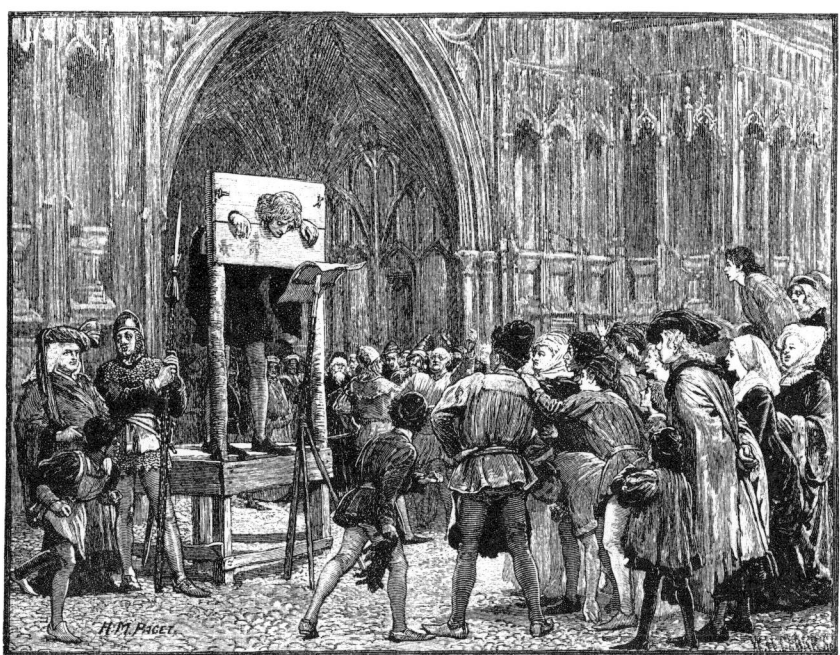

Perkin Warbeck at the pillory

Counterfeit Kings ...

The campaign was a fiasco. Warbeck's forces were easily defeated by the king's army, and he was captured. He was forced to make a full confession and was then paraded through the streets of London before being imprisoned in the Tower in a cell close to that of the Earl of Warwick.

When a third pretender appeared on the scene, Henry decided that the time had come to settle the problem once and for all. Warbeck and Warwick were accused of plotting the king's downfall and they were both sentenced to death. Perkin Warbeck was hanged, drawn and quartered at Tyburn on 23 November 1499. Five days later, the Earl of Warwick was beheaded on Tower Hill. He had spent all but the first nine years of his life in prison simply because he was the nephew of a king.

It had been comparatively easy for Lambert Simnel and Perkin Warbeck to convince people that they were genuine. In the fifteenth century few people ever saw members of the royal family and, because there was no television and no photography, most people did not even know what the king looked like. Besides, both the Earl of Warwick and the young Duke of York had been children when they disappeared, and this made the task of the pretenders much easier. Royal impostors in our own century have faced much greater problems. Far more is known now about the lives and habits of royalty, and photographs show us what they look like. All the same, many people have tried to impersonate princes and princesses in recent times, though none have completely succeeded. There is one case, though, that has puzzled and mystified experts for the last fifty years. The central character in this story is a woman known as Anna Anderson who claims that she is the Grand Duchess Anastasia, youngest daughter of the last Tsar of Russia.

The story begins in Berlin in 1920 when a brief bulletin was published by the police on 18 February:

Yesterday evening at 9 p.m. a girl of about twenty jumped off the Bendler Bridge into the Landwehr Canal with the intention of taking her own life. She was saved by a police sergeant and admitted to the Elisabeth Hospital in Lützowstrasse. No papers or valuables of any kind were found in her possession, and she refused to make any statements about herself or her motives for attempting suicide.

Forgers

The young woman could not or would not speak and it was impossible for doctors or the police to find out who she was. She was sent to a mental hospital and it was there that rumours began to circulate that she was one of the daughters of Tsar Nicholas II. The Tsar and his wife, together with their son and four daughters, had all been murdered in 1918 during the Russian Revolution. Could one of the daughters have survived?

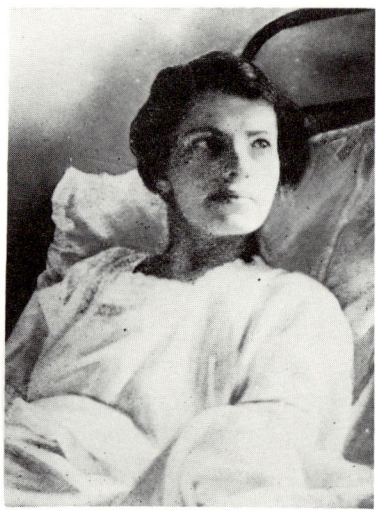

Anna Anderson

Grand Duchess Anastasia

It was not until 1922 that the mysterious woman announced that she was indeed the Grand Duchess Anastasia. She said that she had been wounded in the massacre of her family, and that a soldier called Alexander Tschaikowsky had rescued her and carried her to safety. The woman's claim was believed by some but doubted by many. She was not the first person to have claimed to be Anastasia, and several women have pretended to be one or other of her sisters as well. The Tsar's young son, Alexei, has been the most popular subject for impostors: the first one appeared in 1919 and, as recently as 1960, a man claiming to be the Tsar's son turned up in Berlin. But, from the very beginning, it was clear that the unknown girl was no ordinary impostor. Relations of the Russian royal family went to see her. Many recognized her as Anastasia but others, including her aunt and her tutor, denied that she was the Grand Duchess. Her enemies went to great lengths to prove that she could not possibly be Anastasia but all their attempts failed – her knowledge of Anastasia and of minor details of life in the Russian court could not be faulted. And there was other convincing evidence, too. The mysterious woman had scars that could have resulted from a bullet wound and she had a malformed toe that exactly matched that of the Grand Duchess. Anastasia's middle finger had been the same length as her ring and index fingers; the unknown woman shared this peculiarity. A handwriting expert testified that the claimant's writing and that of Anastasia were identical.

The claimant later travelled to the United States to visit her supporters there and it was then that she adopted the name Anna Anderson in order to shake off persistent reporters. Her friends encouraged her to take her claim to court and she returned to Europe. Anna Anderson's enemies insisted that she was hoping to inherit a vast fortune which the Tsar was supposed to have deposited in the Bank of England. It is unlikely that there is such a fortune but Anna persisted in her claim and the legal battle is still continuing. She now lives in Charlottesville, Virginia, where she is married to a university professor.

Is Anna Anderson an impostor? If she is, then how did she manage to convince so many eminent people, including relatives who had known Anastasia before her supposed death? How did she come to know so much about Anastasia's life, particularly the small details that she could not have read in books? How could she have acquired the amazing physical similarities to the Grand Duchess? Why did her enemies go to such desperate lengths to prove that she was an impostor? And, if Anna Anderson is not Anastasia, then who is she?

These questions will probably never be answered. Anna Anderson is now in her seventies and, when she dies, the solution to the mystery may never be known. If she is an impostor, then she has been the most successful human fraud ever known. To maintain such a deception for fifty years is a remarkable achievement in itself, and it seems impossible that an unknown woman could have known so much about Anastasia or have possessed the same physical peculiarities as the Tsar's daughter. Whatever the truth may be, I like to think that Her Imperial Highness the Grand Duchess Anastasia Nikolayevna is indeed alive and well and living in Charlottesville, Virginia.

6 ... *and Perfect Gentlemen*

The human fakes who impersonate real people have a remarkably difficult and daring task. But there is another kind of human forgery which requires even more skill and courage than that demanded of ordinary impostors. These are the people who, for whatever reason, attempt to live as members of the opposite sex. There are many cases of men who have posed as women, and women who have disguised themselves as men, but perhaps the most extraordinary of all are those of Christian Davies, Hannah Snell and James Barry. What makes their stories so amazing is that they were all women who succeeded in living as men in that most masculine of all worlds – the British army.

Christian Davies was born in Dublin in 1667. She was brought up on a farm where she learned to love horses and country life. When she inherited an aunt's property she was able to manage her own farm, and she appointed a young man called Richard Welsh to run the place for her. According to Christian, Welsh was 'handsome in appearance with a manly face, an open temper, sober and active in business, and a man any woman might love'. And love him Christian did. She and Richard married, had two children and were happy – for a time.

One day Richard left home and never returned. Christian, distraught with worry, tried to manage the farm as best she could while she waited for news of her missing husband. And then, a year later, a letter arrived from Richard. He told her that he had gone to an inn with a stranger, had rather too much to drink, and then had woken up on a ship carrying troops to Holland to fight in the war against France and Spain. When they arrived, he had tried to find a ship to take him home but, as he had no money, he had been forced to enlist in the Duke of Marlborough's armies.

It was a strange story, and an unconvincing one. And why had Richard waited a year before writing to his wife? Christian

... and Perfect Gentlemen

decided to find out for herself. She left her children with relatives, bought a wig and a sword, cut her hair short, and dressed in her husband's clothes. Then she set out to join the army herself. She was accepted, enrolled under the name Christopher Welsh, and was sent to Holland.

Christian seems to have been an ideal recruit. She was praised for her smartness and aptitude and completed her training successfully. Soon she was to see active service against the French. She was wounded in the leg and later captured, only to be freed in exchange for French prisoners. These events did not discourage

Christian. In fact, they seem to have increased her liking for army life. She played the part so well that she was challenged to a duel by a sergeant who thought that she was trying to steal his girlfriend. Christian later described the fight:

> The first thrust I made gave him a slanting wound in his right breast which well nigh finished the business. He returned this with a long gash in my right arm, but before he could recover his guard I gave him a thrust in the right thigh about half a span from the 'Pope's eye'. The next pass he aimed at my breast, but it hit my right arm, though it was little more than a prick of a pin. He then grew weak with loss of the blood which now flowed plentifully from his wound.

Christian survived the duel and further battles against the French. And then, at last, she found Richard. She wrote later:

> I saluted him by name, adding that I had the advantage, for I found I knew him although I appeared to be a stranger to him. 'Sir,' I said, 'you are not unknown to me. Pray when did you last hear from your wife and children?'
> 'Sir,' he replied, 'I have heard no news of them these twelve years though I have written no less than a dozen letters to her which I am apt to believe have miscarried.'
> 'There are many pretty girls here, no doubt, who served to compensate for her absence,' I remarked.
> 'Sir,' he replied, 'you take me for a villain and you lie.'
> A sudden tremor seized me of which he who had his hand on his sword took notice, and looking in my face more intently he stepped forward crying: 'Oh heavens! Is this possible? Can I believe my eyes or is it a delusion? Do I really see my dear Christian?' He clasped me in his arms, kissed me in rapture and bedewed my cheeks with tears of joy.

Christian had found her husband but she liked army life so much that she was reluctant to leave it. She and Richard agreed to pose as brothers but they were not able to keep their secret for long. Christian fractured her skull at the Battle of Ramillies and army surgeons discovered that she was really a woman. She stayed with the regiment for a while but, when Richard was killed in action, she returned to London where she opened a pub in Paddington. The story of her adventures was widely known by now, and her business prospered as a result. Christian died at the age of 108 in Chelsea Hospital and was buried in the grounds with full military honours, as she deserved.

... and Perfect Gentlemen

Like Christian Davies, Hannah Snell joined the army to find her husband. She was married in 1743 to a Dutchman who deserted her shortly afterwards. Their marriage had not been happy but Hannah was determined to find him all the same. She joined the army during a recruiting campaign in Coventry and was enrolled under the name James Gray. Unlike Christian, Hannah was not a model soldier. She received five hundred lashes for neglect of duty and deserted shortly afterwards to avoid being recognized by an acquaintance who enlisted in her regiment.

Hannah Snell in a brawl in a public house

Hannah now decided to search for her husband abroad and she joined the navy. She sailed for the West Indies on the sloop *Swallow* to take part in the campaign against the French. Her shipmates made fun of her at first, calling her 'Miss Molly Gray' because of her effeminacy, but she managed to escape detection and served with courage and initiative in a number of battles. When, at last, she heard reliable news that her husband had been executed for murder in Genoa, Hannah left the navy for good.

The story of Hannah's masquerade soon became public knowledge and she decided to exploit her notoriety by going on the stage. For a while she acted in a series of comic operas at the Royalty Theatre and Sadler's Wells, usually playing the parts of soldiers or sailors. When Hannah left the theatre she found it hard to stop wearing men's clothes. In the end, like Christian Davies before her, she opened a pub. It was called *The Widow in Masquerade or the Female Warrior* and it attracted customers who were anxious to meet the celebrated impostor. The last years of Hannah's life were blighted by mental illness and she died in a lunatic asylum at the age of sixty-nine. She, too, lies buried in the grounds of Chelsea Hospital.

In Kensal Green Cemetery in north London another extraordinary woman lies buried. The inscription on the battered and broken gravestone reads:

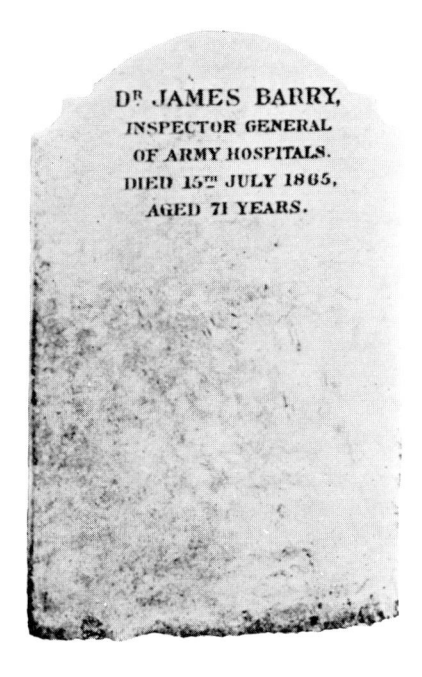

> Dʀ JAMES BARRY,
> INSPECTOR GENERAL
> OF ARMY HOSPITALS.
> DIED 15ᵀᴴ JULY 1865,
> AGED 71 YEARS.

Unlike Christian Davies and Hannah Snell, James Barry lived as a man for almost all her life and the secret of her true sex was only discovered after her death.

It is impossible to say who James Barry really was. Various theories have been put forward – including a suggestion that she was an illegitimate child of George IV – but the most convincing is that she was a niece of the celebrated artist, James Barry. He and his eminent friends certainly took a very great interest in the child who soon proved to have outstanding intellectual capabilities. But how could she be educated? Women were not allowed to go to university at that time and, no matter how brilliant a girl might be, the most she could hope for was a career as a governess. The solution was simple – and daring. If the young genius could not attend university as a female, then she would have to go there as a male. And so, in 1809 at the age of ten, James Barry (as she was now to be called) enrolled as a medical student at Edinburgh University, dressed as a boy.

At Edinburgh, Barry avoided the social life enjoyed by the other students. She could not risk detection; all she could do was read and study. At the age of twelve, she qualified as a doctor, proving to herself, if not to the world, that women are the intellectual equals of men. But she was to pay a terrible price for this achievement. She had qualified as a doctor disguised as a man and she would have to remain a man in order to practice her profession.

After working at St Thomas' Hospital in London for a while, Dr James Barry enlisted as an army surgeon and in 1816, aged seventeen, she sailed for Cape Town. At the Cape, and during the rest of her career, Barry demonstrated both a brilliant skill as a surgeon and a dedicated zeal to reform the army medical services. And, especially at Cape Town, she led an active social life. Mark Twain heard about her when he later visited South Africa:

> There were plenty of pretty girls, but none of them caught [Barry], none of them could get hold of his heart; evidently he was not a marrying man. And that was another marvel, another puzzle, and made no end of perplexing talk. Once he was called in the night, on obstetric service, to do what he could for a woman who was believed to be dying. He was prompt and scientific, and saved both mother and child. There are other instances on record which testify to his mastership of his

profession; and many which testify to his love of it, and his devotion to it. Among other adventures of his was a duel of a desperate sort, fought with swords, at the Castle. He killed his man.

Twain was wrong: Barry did fight a duel but she did not kill her opponent.

It seems surprising that Barry's secret was never discovered during her lifetime. There was certainly a great deal of gossip about her and she was often teased for her effeminacy. But she would react violently to any slur on her 'masculinity', and the idea that the brilliant doctor could possibly be a woman seemed preposterous in the early nineteenth century.

As she grew older, Barry became increasingly odd and eccentric. But her brilliance as a surgeon and as a medical reformer never wavered. From the Cape, she was transferred to Jamaica and then to St Helena, Malta, Corfu and Canada. In each place she antagonized the authorities by her insistence on the highest standards of medical care. In 1864 she returned to London and died the following year. It was only then that her sad secret was revealed at last: the charwoman who laid out her body announced that Barry was a woman.

Dr James Barry died in 1865. In that same year, by an ironic coincidence, Elizabeth Garrett Anderson became the 'first' woman doctor in Great Britain.

7 · 'Mincemeat swallowed whole'

In the graveyard of the southern Spanish town of Huelva, an Englishman lies buried. The inscription on the tombstone is simple: 'William Martin. Born 29th March, 1907. Died 24th April, 1943. *Dulce et decorum est pro patria mori. R.I.P.*' Few of the people who pass the grave today will know the extraordinary story which lies behind this simple tribute, or realize that William Martin played a vital part in one of the most astonishing deceptions of the Second World War. Any passer-by who wonders idly who the dead man was and how he came to be buried in a small Spanish town would be very surprised to learn that he had never existed at all. For William Martin was, in fact, a fake, 'the man who never was'.

The story starts in the autumn of 1942 when the Allied forces had gained control of North Africa from the Germans and the Italians. The British and the Americans were anxious to gain a foothold in Europe and it was clear that such an attack would be best launched from the African coast. The obvious course was to invade the island of Sicily and strike from there at the heart of southern Europe. But, if this plan was obvious to the Allies, then it would certainly be obvious to the Germans as well. How could the Allies disguise their intentions from the enemy? Could they persuade the Germans that the attack was to be made in another place altogether?

It was then that a British Intelligence officer had a brilliant idea. Why not find a dead body, disguise it as a serving officer, and give it documents showing that the attack was to be made somewhere else? Then float the body ashore on the Spanish coast so that it would look as though the man had died in a plane crash. Spain was a neutral country but German agents there would investigate the body and examine the documents he carried. With any luck, the Germans would be taken in by the deception and not bother to reinforce the defences of Sicily. The idea was fantastic but there was every chance that it might succeed. And so the plan went ahead for Operation Mincemeat, as it was to be called.

The biggest problem at first was where to find a body. Normally this would have been easy enough – especially during wartime – but the corpse had to be chosen with care. It had to give the appearance of having died from drowning or else from the exposure and shock that would result from a plane crash in the sea. At last a suitable corpse was found, that of a young man who had died from pneumonia following exposure. His relatives gave their permission for the body to be used on the strict condition that the young man's identity should never be revealed.

Other problems were easier to solve. It was decided to place the body in the sea near Huelva. Research showed that the weather and the tides would be favourable on that stretch of coast, and there was a German agent in the town who would be sure to hear the news when the body was washed ashore. It would be launched from a submarine as this was the only way it could be placed close to land without detection.

The person and the place had been decided. The planners now turned their attention to the most vital part of the entire operation: the document which would persuade the Germans that the Allies were not going to invade Sicily. This took the form of a letter from the Vice-Chief of the Imperial General Staff to the general commanding the army in Tunisia, telling him that the intention was to invade Sardinia and Corsica. The letter contained a daring double-bluff: it said that the British were going to make the Germans believe that Sicily was the target! Other letters were included, too, in order to establish why the dead officer should be carrying such an important document. It was decided to make him an expert in the use of invasion landing craft. This would explain why he was flying to North Africa, and letters from Lord Mountbatten to the Commander-in-Chief of the Mediterranean and to General Eisenhower were written to substantiate it.

It was now time to give 'the man who never was' an identity. The Germans would only be deceived by the documents if the man who carried them was clearly genuine. And so he was given a name, William Martin, and Intelligence forgers set to work in order to provide him with the personal details that would create a

'Mincemeat swallowed whole'

convincing personality. It was easy enough to obtain an identity card for Major Martin but not so easy to find a photograph for it. They tried taking a picture of the corpse but this didn't look convincing. Then, quite by chance, they came across someone who looked just like the dead man and photographed him instead. Then the forgers turned their attention to the papers and belongings that an officer would be likely to carry: a photograph of his fiancée, letters from her and from his father, a letter from his bank manager complaining about Major Martin's overdraft, bills, receipts, theatre ticket stubs – all the minor paraphernalia of a man's wallet. These papers were carefully aged in order to look realistically worn, and to them were added the small but important items that a man collects in his pockets: coins, old bus tickets, matches, keys, a pencil. Major Martin was now ready to make his journey.

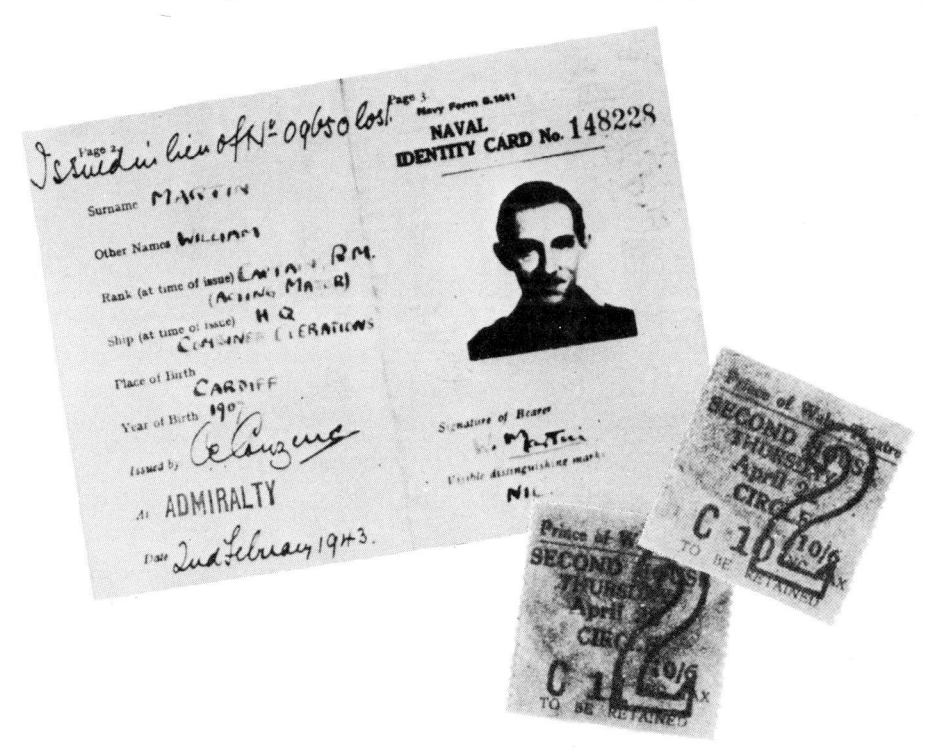

On 19 April 1943 the submarine *Seraph* sailed from Holy Loch for Malta, carrying with it a canister containing the body of Major Martin. At 4.30 a.m. on 30 April the *Seraph* surfaced off the

Major Martin's fiancée

mouth of the Huelva river. The canister was unlocked and the body released from its vacuum coffin. The commander quickly checked to make sure that all was in order and then he and his officers murmured prayers from the burial service. Then the body was given a gentle push into the sea. Soon, Major Martin was drifting inshore with the tide. Operation Mincemeat had been completed.

On 3 May, British Intelligence received a report from the Naval Attaché in Spain to say that the body of a Major Martin had been found by a fisherman on 30 April, and that he had been given a full military funeral. But what had happened to the documents? These had been passed to the Spanish authorities but they were eventually returned to London where Intelligence experts anxiously examined them. Only now could they tell whether Operation Mincemeat had worked, and whether Major Martin had succeeded in his strange mission. The letters appeared to be unopened when they arrived in London and the seals on the envelopes were still intact. But close examination soon revealed that the envelopes had indeed been tampered with and that someone had read and copied the contents. A message was immediately sent to the prime minister, Winston Churchill, who was then in Washington. It simply read: 'Mincemeat swallowed whole.'

But, even though the letters had been opened, no one could be quite sure that the Germans had been completely taken in. Then, as the date for the Allied invasion of Sicily drew near, reports came through that the enemy had diverted their defence efforts from the south of the island. Major Martin had indeed succeeded in his mission. If he had failed, then many hundreds of British and American lives would have been lost in the invasion.

The final proof of the success of the operation came after the war was over. A search of captured German naval archives revealed copies of the documents that Major Martin had carried, and German Intelligence reports which showed that Operation Mincemeat had indeed been swallowed whole. The unknown man in the grave at Huelva would have been proud of the part he played after death in such a spectacular human forgery.

8 · The Piltdown Man

Archaeology has always offered plenty of scope to the hoaxer and the forger. In the time of the Roman Empire collectors paid well for artistic relics of earlier times, especially ancient Greek sculpture and coins, but it was during the nineteenth century that increasing interest in archaeology was accompanied by a rapid growth in forged relics of the past. Collectors were prepared to pay large amounts for antiquities, and forgers were only too happy to meet the demand. Many archaeological objects have little financial value, though, and it is in this area that the hoaxer comes into his own. Time and again people have shown that it is just as easy to fool distinguished experts as it is to dupe people who have no specialized knowledge at all.

Perhaps the most famous archaeological fake of all was the Piltdown Man. No one knows for certain who engineered this spectacular forgery but whoever it was could congratulate themselves on having fooled the experts for over forty years.

The story begins in 1908 when a workman digging for gravel in the Sussex village of Piltdown uncovered an object which looked like a coconut. He smashed it with his pick but kept a piece to show a keen amateur geologist called Charles Dawson. Dawson identified it as a thick piece of bone from a human skull and noted that it seemed to be extremely old. He searched for further pieces but it was not until 1911 that he found four more fragments of bone which appeared to be from the same skull. The following year he showed his finds to Dr Arthur Smith Woodward, then Keeper of the Geological Department at the British Museum, who confirmed that the pieces of bone were very old indeed.

Woodward and Dawson immediately organized digging operations at Piltdown with the help of a young Jesuit priest, Teilhard de Chardin. They found more fragments of skull and then Dawson unearthed the most astonishing find of all: half a lower

The Piltdown skull

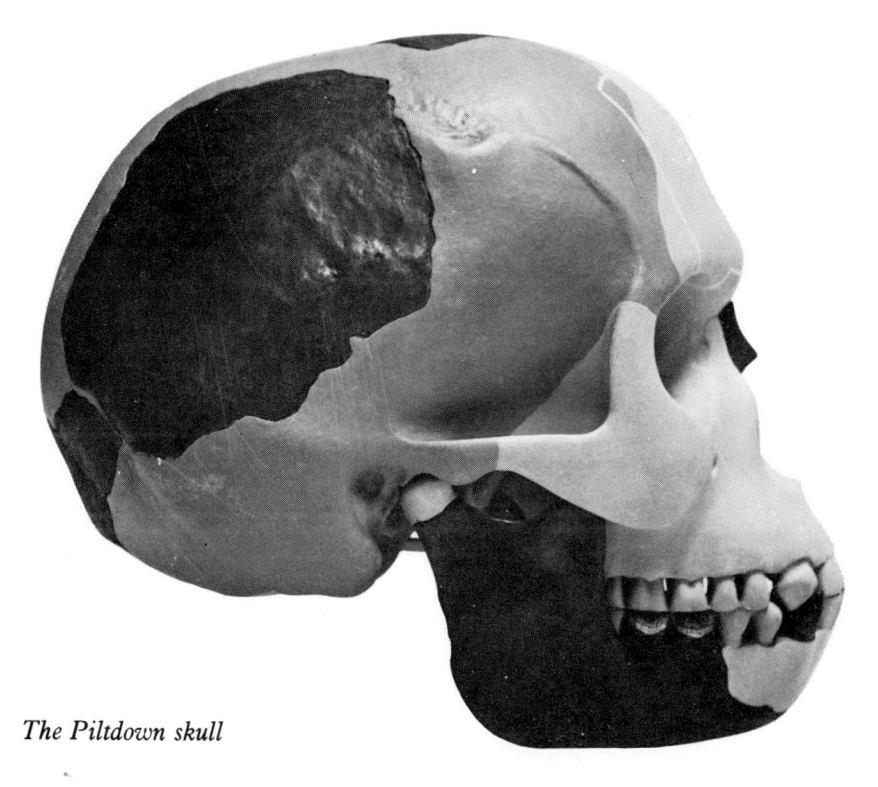

jawbone which contained two teeth. When they examined it, Woodward and Dawson found that the jaw was that of an ape. The teeth, though, were human.

This was an amazing discovery. Ever since Charles Darwin had published his theories about the origin of man, people had believed in the existence of the Missing Link, a creature who had existed on the evolutionary scale between the apes and men. Many hoped that evidence of his existence would be discovered. Now it seemed that the Missing Link had at last been found in the Sussex countryside.

Dawson and his friends were convinced that their finds did indeed point to the existence of a creature who combined the characteristics of ape and man, and the fact that a skull could be reconstructed from the bone fragments and jaw seemed to prove it beyond a doubt. They reported their discovery to a meeting of the Geological Society in December 1912.

The response was overwhelming. Although a few scientists remained unconvinced, most shared Dawson's theory about his

Experts examine the Piltdown skull. Charles Dawson is standing second from right (portrait by J. Cooke).

discovery. The Missing Link was given an official scientific name: *Eoanthropus Dawsoni*, or the Dawson Dawn Man. The news excited not only scientists but the public as well. Coach parties were organized to visit the site of the discoveries and the local pub was hastily renamed The Piltdown Man. Flocks of expert palaeontologists and geologists rushed to Piltdown to observe the diggings which continued for the next three years. National pride played a substantial part in the acclaim given to the Piltdown finds – all previous important discoveries about man's ancestry had been made abroad, in Java, France and Germany. Britain had now beaten the foreigners at their own game.

Further finds at Piltdown seemed to confirm the Dawn Man theory. Teilhard de Chardin unearthed a human canine tooth which fitted into the jaw and, in 1914 and 1915, Dawson himself found more pieces of the skull, together with fossils, implements and relics of prehistoric animals. He died in 1917, happy in the knowledge that he had made an important contribution to the study of the evolution of man.

The Piltdown Man

Others were not so sure. As the years passed, opposition to the Piltdown Man grew. It was not until 1948, though, that steps were taken to solve the mystery once and for all. During the forty years since the first bone had been found at Piltdown, sophisticated scientific tests had been developed. The British Museum authorities now agreed to these being applied to the Piltdown finds.

Dr Kenneth Page Oakley subjected the skull fragments to a fluorine test which he had developed for discovering the age of bones. He found that the skull was only fifty thousand years old instead of the five hundred thousand that had previously been thought. The news startled scientists but made little impression on the general public. After all, what difference could a few hundred thousand years make? The Piltdown skull was very old. That was all that mattered.

More tests were carried out in 1953 and it was these which shocked the country and the world. It was found that both the jaw and the teeth had come from a modern orang-utan. The teeth had been filed to make them look human, and they had been stained with oil paint to give the appearance of age. There had been a smell of burning when the scientists drilled a hole in the jaw. This would not have happened with ancient bone, and the results of a simple test thus hammered another nail in the Dawn Man's coffin. Further examination showed that all the objects found at Piltdown were fakes. The skull fragments were indeed old but they were not as old as Dawson had claimed and they certainly had not been at Piltdown for very long.

The Piltdown Man was completely discredited, and the press seized upon the story with delight. 'Great Missing Link Hoax Rocks Scientists', 'Experts were Spoofed by a Monkey's Jaw' and 'All the World Laughs at the Piltdown Man' were just three of the headlines on the day the news was released. And it *was* a good story. People always enjoy seeing experts fooled and they relished the discomfiture of the eminent authorities who had believed for so long in the authenticity of the Piltdown Man.

Who was responsible for the hoax? All the evidence seemed to point to Charles Dawson, the unassuming country solicitor who had found the first fragments of bone. But he had died in 1917 and could not answer the charges. Many people sprang to his defence and it does indeed seem unlikely that he would have had the detailed knowledge of geology, anatomy, chemistry and prehistoric archaeology needed to organize such a detailed and convincing fake. If he *was* responsible, then he must have had an accomplice. Recent evidence has suggested that this accomplice might have been William Johnson Sollas, Professor of Geology at Oxford University, who organized the hoax in order to make a fool of his old enemy, Dr Woodward. There is also evidence to suggest that Teilhard de Chardin was responsible for the fakes, either alone or with the help of Professor Sollas. Even now, seventy years after the first fragments of bone were found, the mystery of the Piltdown Man continues to puzzle the experts. We may never know the truth.

When Dawson died, his private collection of geological specimens was presented to the Hastings Museum. In 1954 it was discovered that many of the items were forgeries too. Among them were flint implements supposed to have been found in Sussex but which had really been made by one of the most famous forgers of the nineteenth century – Flint Jack.

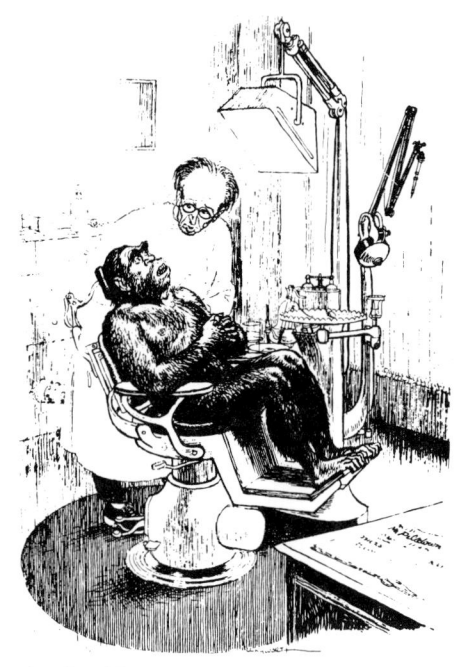

Dawn man at the dentist, 'I am sorry I shall have to extract the whole of the lower jaw.'

9 · Flint Jack

One evening in 1862 a gathering of distinguished geologists and their wives assembled in a fashionable lecture room in Cavendish Square, London. They were all members of the Geologists' Association, and they had been invited to hear an address from their Vice-President on ancient flint implements. The room soon became crowded and, before long, every seat had been taken except for those in the front row which had been reserved for the President and the committee. The members talked among themselves as they waited for the speaker to arrive and then, suddenly, a silence fell as a very strange-looking man came into the room. So odd was his appearance in comparison with the elegant clothes of the audience that one or two people laughed out loud. Then their laughter changed to gasps of horror as the new arrival made his way to the front of the hall and calmly sat down on one of the reserved seats. The *People's Magazine* reported later:

> He was a weather-beaten man of about 45 years of age and he came in dirty, tattered clothes, and heavy navvy's boots, to take precedence of the whole assemblage ... He wore a dark cloth coat, hanging in not unpicturesque rags about the elbows; it was unbuttoned over a cotton shirt which might once have been white, but which had degenerated to a yellow brown. About his neck was a fragment of a blue cotton handkerchief; his skin was of a gipsy brown, his hair hung in lank black locks about a forehead and face that was not altogether unprepossessing, except for the furtive and cunning glances which he occasionally cast around him from eyes that did not correspond with each other in size and expression. His corduroys, which were in a very sorry condition, had been turned up; and their owner had evidently travelled through heavy clay, the dried remains of which bedaubed his boots.

It is hardly surprising that the eminent members of the Geologists' Association were taken aback by the appearance of this man at their meeting. Their bewilderment only increased when the President and committee arrived and sat down beside the stranger without giving him a second glance.

The Vice-President then stood up and gave his lecture. The mysterious stranger listened with great interest and appeared from his expression to be very knowledgeable about the subject himself. The speaker concluded his talk with some remarks about modern forgeries of ancient flint weapons and it was then that the identity of the stranger was revealed at last. The Vice-President announced that there was a person in the audience who, with the aid of a small piece of bent iron rod, could produce on demand flint weapons that would look just like genuine Stone Age relics.

Flint Jack

He invited the stranger to mount the platform. The man did so, and produced some pieces of flint from his pocket. He selected one and gave it a few careless blows with what appeared to be a crooked nail. Within a few minutes he had produced a small arrow-head. The audience gathered round to watch in amazement as the stranger went on to make more arrow-heads which he then sold to them for sixpence each. Finally, having exhausted his stock of flints, the man left the hall. This time there was no laughter as he made his way through the audience.

The man who had so amazed the Geologists' Association was none other than Edward Simpson, one of the most gifted forgers of the nineteenth century. He was usually known as Flint Jack, though he had a variety of other nicknames, including Fossil Willy, Cockney Bill, Bones, Shirtless, Snake Billy and Old Antiquarian. He specialized in the forgery of Stone Age arrow-heads, although he also made fake fossils, pottery, inscribed stones, and brooches. Flint Jack was a master of archaeological forgery but he was more than just another crook out to make easy money. He was a craftsman and an artist, and he combined a wide knowledge of archaeology and geology with a genuine interest and affection for the subject. His fakes were remarkably convincing, and he always prided himself on the fact that the British Museum had several of his forgeries on display!

Flint Jack was born near Whitby, Yorkshire, in 1815, the son of a sailor. When he was fourteen he went to work for a local geologist and it was from him that Jack acquired his love of antiquities and his fascination for geology. He started to collect his own fossils and later began to sell them to the many dealers who then existed to cater to the popular demand for ancient relics. The Victorians were insatiable collectors, particularly of antiquities. They weren't especially interested in the artistic or historical significance of the objects they collected; all they asked was that the objects should be as *old* as possible. This attitude was a great help to Flint Jack when he came to sell his forgeries, for it meant that few people were able to tell whether his work was genuine or not. On the other hand, it also meant that his own craftsmanship went unrecognized.

It was a corrupt dealer who first encouraged Jack to forge his own arrow-heads in 1843. Jack did this so well that he was soon

Forgers

turning out scores of flints. He was able to sell these easily and then turned his attention to more elaborate forgeries. He made urns and stone implements in a home-made kiln and then decided to make armour as well. His first successful piece of fake armour was a Roman breastplate which he made out of an old tin tray and sold for a handsome sum in Scarborough. Seals and inscribed stones followed, all of which were snapped up by eager antiquarians.

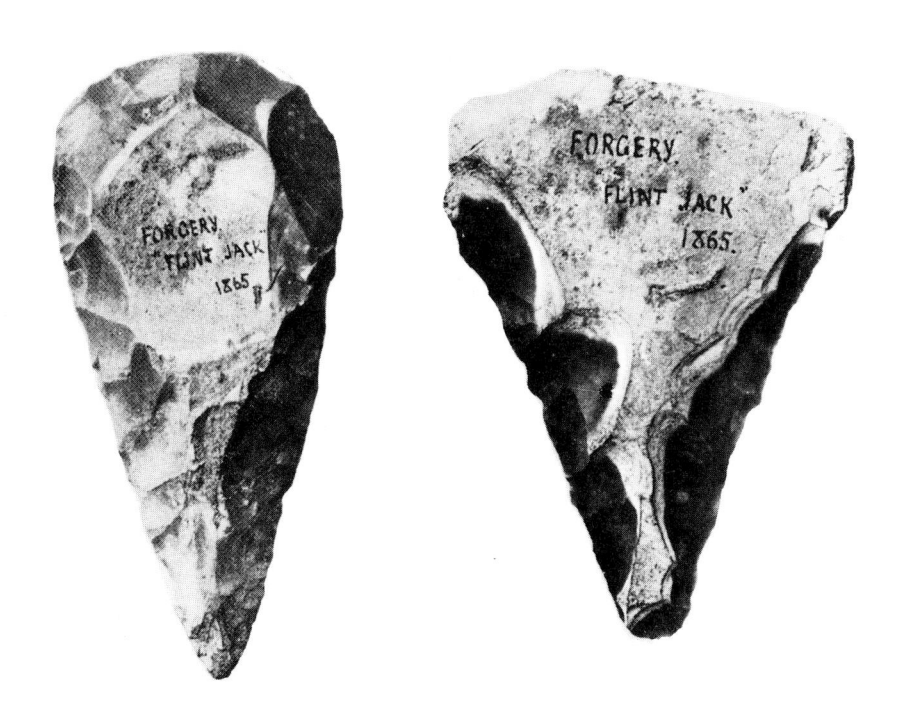

Jack then began to move south, forging happily as he went. By the time he arrived in London he was drinking heavily and was forced to produce more and more forgeries to pay for this weakness. He sold great quantities of forged flints to London dealers and it was not long before there were so many on the market that he was forced to move on in case he was detected. His later wanderings took him all over England: he sold fake flints in Northampton and Newcastle, rings and beads in Liverpool and the Lake District, and fossils in Birmingham and Sheffield.

Jack was often accused of forging his relics and he always admitted this when challenged. On one occasion, a friend asked his opinion about a collection of flints which he had bought from a dealer. Jack told him that not only were they forgeries but that he himself had made them! It is this honesty which makes Flint Jack such an attractive and disarming character. He was not the dissolute and deceitful criminal that his enemies branded him. He merely made copies of genuine antiquities. Was he to blame if his skill and craftsmanship led people to think that they were genuine?

It was this honesty – and his dedication to alcohol – which led to Jack's downfall. By the time he gave his demonstration to the Geologists' Association the full story of his fakes was known. He was the most famous forger in the kingdom but his livelihood had gone. Everyone knew who he was and what he had done. No one would buy flints or fossils from him now.

By 1867 Flint Jack was destitute, forced to beg from friends for food and, of course, drink. In January his friend James Wyatt noted in his diary that Jack had borrowed sixpence from him. Wyatt wrote:

> It appears that he proceeded to the last house on the London Road but unfortunately that is a public house and he could not resist the temptation of entering. The consequence was that he got drunk, and as the craving increased after his money was gone he came back to the town, opened the front door of a house near mine, and took a barometer, but having been seen by a man outside he bolted and threw the barometer away. Later in the evening, finding a light in the school-room attached to the Methodist Chapel he entered and stole the clock, which he tried to sell to the keeper of a public house, and finally left it with him as a deposit. The police got on the scent and ran him down at a low lodging-house, and then removed him to the lock-up.

Flint Jack was tried on 11 March 1867 and sentenced to one year's imprisonment in Bedford gaol. One of his friends visited him there and later published an appeal to the public for help when the time came for Jack to be released.

> The man possesses more real practical antiquarian knowledge than many of the leading antiquarian writers of the day; and he is a good geologist and palaeontologist. Is it meet, then, that he should be allowed

to starve when a few mites from those whom he may have duped, but whom, at all events, he has ultimately benefitted by his open disclosure, and by his indomitable skill, would materially assist him, and perhaps turn his talents into a better and honourable channel?

But Victorian collectors could not forget how they had been duped, and they refused to forgive and forget Flint Jack's fakes. They weren't interested in the quality or scientific value of his work; to them, he was nothing but a common criminal. Had he lived in our own time, Flint Jack might have made a valuable contribution to the study of archaeology. As it was, he could only express himself by forging the relics he loved so much.

10 · The Marvellous Boy

On a warm August evening in 1770, a destitute young man called Thomas Chatterton climbed the stairs to his attic room in the Holborn district of London. He closed the door behind him and then began to tear a pile of manuscripts into small pieces. Having done this, Chatterton poured himself a drink of water and added to it a dose of the deadly poison arsenic. He drained the glass and then lay down on his bed. The next morning his landlady found him. The boy was dead, his body contorted with agony and covered with vomit. He was only seventeen years old.

Later, when the story of Chatterton's sad life and astonishing forgeries became widely known, people were to ignore the depressing details of his miserable and lonely death. He became a symbol of neglected genius, a romantic image of a beautiful young poet ignored and abandoned by a world that failed to recognize his true worth. Artists painted sentimental pictures of his final moments, poets honoured his literary achievement in verse, and plays and operas were based on his life. While he lived Chatterton had yearned for such recognition and attention but he was only to receive it after death.

The life that was to end so sadly in a Holborn attic began in Bristol in 1753. Chatterton's father was a schoolmaster but he died before his son was born, leaving his wife penniless with two children to support. Chatterton was a difficult and moody child but a clever one. He learned to read very young and eagerly devoured books on heraldry, music and astronomy. At the age of eight he was given a place at Colston's Hospital, a charity school for boys who were to become apprentices. It was perhaps here that Chatterton's fascination for the Middle Ages first grew: the school was housed in an ancient building that was once a priory, and the school uniform of long coat, yellow stockings and partly shaven head was mediaeval in appearance.

Chatterton left school when he was fourteen and became apprenticed to a local lawyer. His work was very dull – it consisted of copying legal documents – but he led a full life in the evenings. He was already a promising poet and many of his early verses were written for the local girls he met after work. But, although he enjoyed an active social life, Chatterton was ambitious. He knew that he was a good poet. How could he achieve the success and recognition he felt sure he deserved?

The answer lay in the ancient church of St Mary Redcliffe. Chatterton spent hours there, gazing at the mediaeval tombs and carvings, and he became increasingly obsessed with the life and history of the Middle Ages. He decided to invent a fifteenth-century priest and poet, and produce manuscripts of poems supposed to have been written by him. And so Thomas Rowley was born.

Chatterton's uncle was a sexton at the church and, because of the family connection, his father had been allowed to bring old documents home to use for covering schoolbooks and for lighting fires. Such treatment of ancient manuscripts seems incredible to us today but, in the eighteenth century, few people cared about preserving the records of the past. Some of these manuscripts were still lying about the house and it was on these that Chatterton wrote his Rowley forgeries. His first document was a supposed account of the opening of a bridge. Chatterton announced that he had found the manuscript in the church, and it created a great deal of interest. Inspired by this attention, he went on to produce poems and fragments of plays which he claimed had been written by Thomas Rowley in the fifteenth century. They were written in a pseudo-mediaeval style which seemed genuine enough to the local experts who examined them:

> When Freedom dreste, yn blodde steyned veste
> To everie knyghte her warre songe sunge
> Uponne her hedde, wyld wedes were spredde,
> A gorie anlace bye her honge ...

The language of such poems was not authentic, though. They were inspired not by mediaeval poets but by Shakespeare and Spenser, and Chatterton either invented mediaeval words of his own or else found them in dictionaries. But the poems certainly *looked* genuine to the Bristol antiquarians, who welcomed them as unique discoveries.

As Chatterton became more obsessed with his creation, he decided that local acclaim was not enough. Thomas Rowley's poems deserved a wider and more illustrious readership. He sent copies of some of the poems to Horace Walpole, a celebrated writer and connoisseur. Walpole expressed interest and asked to see more, with a view to possible publication of the work of the unknown fifteenth-century priest that Chatterton had discovered. Excited at the prospect of escape from the provincial life of Bristol, Chatterton then overplayed his hand. He sent further poems but he made the mistake of telling Walpole that he was a sixteen-year-old apprentice and that he would like a job in London. Walpole's suspicions were aroused by this, and he showed the manuscripts to the poet Thomas Gray who immediately pronounced them to be forgeries. Walpole told Chatterton that he wanted nothing more to do with him or with Thomas Rowley, and he advised the boy to persevere with his legal studies.

Chatterton's disappointment was intense. He felt sure that he had been rejected because of his youth and because he was poor. His reply to Walpole was bitter:

Though I am but sixteen years of age I have lived long enough to see that poverty attends literature. I am obliged to you, sir, for your advice and will go a little beyond it, by destroying all my useless lumber of literature and by never using my pen but in the law.

Walpole had not returned the poems with his letter, and Chatterton was forced to write to him again:

I cannot reconcile your behaviour to me with the notions I once entertained of you. I think myself injured, sir, and did not you know my circumstances, you would not dare to treat me thus. I have twice sent for a copy of the manuscript – no answer from you. An explanation or excuse for your silence would oblige.

Chatterton's revenge was to come after his death. When people heard about Walpole's rejection of the Rowley poems, he was denounced as the heartless aristocrat who had driven Chatterton to suicide.

Chatterton did not give up hope and, despite his promise to Walpole, he did not stop 'using his pen'. He now concentrated on poems of his own, some of which were published in Bristol newspapers. He knew, though, that local fame was not enough and so he decided to go to London and seek his fortune there. But he was still an apprentice and he was legally bound to remain in the lawyer's office. How could he gain his release? The solution was dramatic and, in the light of what happened later, sadly prophetic: he told his employer that he would kill himself if he was not released from his apprenticeship. The lawyer hastily agreed and Chatterton set off for London, taking with him five pounds and a bundle of unpublished poems.

Chatterton's commemorative handkerchief

But London was to prove another disappointment. Some of his poems were published there but not enough to earn a living. He took lodgings in Holborn, then a very seedy part of London, and became increasingly desperate as poverty and hunger overtook him. In his letters home he bravely disguised his real situation, pretending to the end that he was a success at last:

> I have an universal acquaintance; my company is courted everywhere

Forgers

... The ladies are not out of my acquaintance. I have a deal of business now, and must therefore bid you adieu.

He expressed his true feelings in his last poem, written a day or two before his death:

> Farewell, my mother! – cease my anguished soul,
> Nor let Distraction's billows o'er me roll! –
> Have mercy, Heaven! when here I cease to live,
> And this last act of wretchedness forgive.

The 'last act of wretchedness' took place on 24 August 1770. But after Thomas Chatterton had ended his life, his reputation began to soar. Critics at last recognized the quality of his work and saw, too, that beneath the mock-mediaeval language of the Rowley forgeries lay poems of great worth. From that day to this, poets and painters have been moved by his tragic story and, like William Wordsworth, have been inspired by thoughts of

> ... Chatterton, the marvellous Boy,
> The sleepless soul that perished in his pride.

11 · The Boy Who Wrote a Play by Shakespeare

In 1794, over twenty years after Chatterton died, his tragic life and romantic death still exercised a powerful hold on the imagination. One of the many young people who became obsessed by the poet was William Henry Ireland, the seventeen-year-old son of an

art dealer. Chatterton's story held a particular fascination for William because their circumstances were so similar. William was the same age as Chatterton had been when he died and he, too, was unhappily apprenticed to a lawyer. Like Chatterton, William longed for recognition of his literary gifts but, whereas Chatterton had hoped for public appreciation of his work, William's main concern was to win the approval of his father. Samuel Ireland thought little of his son; he considered the boy to be remarkably stupid and incompetent, fit for nothing better than a life as a lawyer's clerk. Try as he might, William could not convince his father that he was capable of greater things. He compared his own failure with that of Chatterton. They were, he felt, kindred spirits: two legal apprentices of the same age, both born with poetic gifts that the world refused to recognize. William even went so far as to contemplate killing himself as Chatterton had done, but not for long. An alternative solution soon presented itself. Chatterton had forged poems in his efforts to secure fame. William would do the same.

William's father collected rare books and curious objects of all kinds but he was particularly obsessed by Shakespeare. He travelled widely in search of Shakespearian relics and his greatest wish was to own an original manuscript by the great poet. William knew that the surest way of winning his father's approval was by providing a choice addition to his collection.

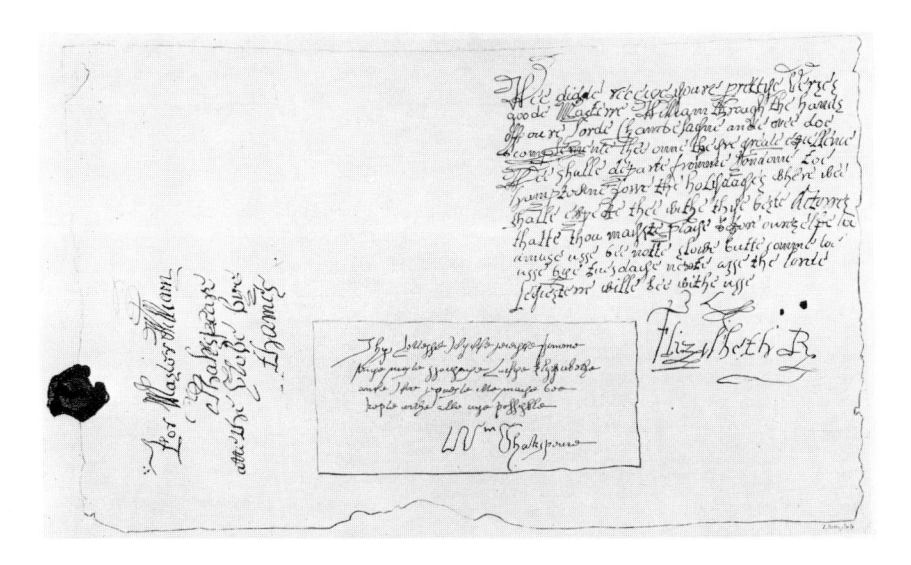

The first forgery was a brief letter by Queen Elizabeth I which William pretended to find in an old book. His father was delighted with it and, inspired by the success of his first venture, William became more ambitious. The second forgery was an ancient lease signed by Shakespeare. William forged the document on parchment which he found in his employer's office, and his handiwork was good enough to fool his father who was overjoyed to possess at last a specimen of his hero's signature. William explained that he had found the document in a chest of ancient manuscripts kept in the attic of a gentleman who wished to remain anonymous. The gentleman was grateful to William for his legal services and had told him to take anything he liked from the chest. The story was unconvincing, to say the least, but Samuel Ireland believed it. After all, his son was much too stupid to even dream of faking a document, let alone be able to forge one himself. The signature was surely genuine.

William revelled in his father's approval. If a mere signature had worked such wonders then surely an entire letter would result in even more lavish praise? And so the anonymous gentleman's mysterious chest began to yield a steady stream of Shakespearian letters and relics: a love letter to Anne Hathaway, a lock of the poet's hair, a self-portrait and even a new version of Shakespeare's will all found their way into the eager hands of Samuel Ireland. The greatest prize of all was a letter to Shakespeare from Queen Elizabeth:

> Wee didde receive your prettye verses good Masterre William through the hands of our Lord Chamberlyne and wee do complemente thee onne thyre great excellence. We shalle departe fromme Londonne toe Hampstowne forre the holydayes where wee shalle expect thee with thy beste actorres that thou mayeste playe before ourselfe toe amuse usse bee note slowe butte come to usse bye Tuesdaye nexte asse the Lord Leycesterre wille be withe usse.
> ELIZABETH R.

Samuel was completely deceived by these finds, as were many of the experts who came to inspect them.

William then announced that he had found in the chest a completely unknown play by Shakespeare called *Vortigern and Rowena*. This time, the anonymous benefactor refused to part with the original manuscript and William would have to copy it out himself. It is hardly surprising that William should have invented this excuse. To write a play by Shakespeare would be difficult enough without making the task even more complicated

Forgers

by forging the original manuscript. He settled down to write *Vortigern and Rowena* while theatre managers vied with each other for the privilege of staging it. Before the play had been finished,

Ireland's forged manuscript of Vortigern and Rowena

The Boy Who Wrote a Play by Shakespeare

the playwright Richard Brinsley Sheridan arranged to produce it at Drury Lane with the greatest Shakespearian actors of the day in the leading parts.

Sheridan was disappointed with *Vortigern and Rowena* when he saw the finished manuscript and so was the great Mrs Siddons, who made an excuse to leave the cast after she had read it. Little did either of them know that the play had been written in two months by a seventeen-year-old boy. *Vortigern and Rowena* may not have been a convincing Shakespeare play but it was, all the same, a remarkable achievement for such a young writer.

The production went ahead despite the doubts of the producer and the public, and the first (and last) performance took place on 2 April 1796. At first all went well but trouble started in the third act when the audience began to laugh at the high voice of one of the actors. And, when the curtain fell on top of a 'dead' actor who then got up and walked away, the performance began to disintegrate completely. By the end of the evening, the actors were guying their parts and the audience were throwing oranges onto the stage.

The public and the critics denounced *Vortigern and Rowena* as a forgery, and denounced, too, the other documents which William had 'found'. Only Samuel Ireland remained convinced that they were genuine. How could his stupid seventeen-year-old son possibly have written a play by Shakespeare? And, even when William himself publicly confessed to the forgeries, Samuel refused to believe him.

William Ireland abandoned forgery after that and decided to support himself with money earned from his own writing. He was never very successful but the fame of his Shakespeare forgeries helped to sell his books. For the rest of his life, he continued to compare himself with Chatterton and he even published a book of poems which were all about him. But William never repeated his early success and he never matched Chatterton's genius. Thomas Chatterton is remembered now as a gifted poet, but William Ireland's fame rests solely on the fact that he was the boy who wrote a play by Shakespeare.

An acrostic on Chatterton's name composed by his admirer and imitator, William Henry Ireland, famous for his Shakespeare forgeries.

Comfort and joy's forever fled
He ne'er will warble more!
Ah me! the sweetest youth is dead
That e'er tun'd reed before.
The hand of Mis'ry bowed him low,
E'en Hope forsook his brain;
Relentless man contemn'd his woe:
To you he sigh'd in vain.
Oppressed with want, in wild despair he cried
'**N**o more I'll live,' swallowed the draught and died.

12 · The Master Forger

People who forge works of art can be divided into two distinct groups. The first of these are the professionals, who paint fake pictures by famous artists to sell to collectors and museums for large sums. Their principal motive is financial, and they use their artistic skills in order to obtain money. The second group is less easy to define. These are the amateur forgers, and their reasons for painting fakes can be much more complicated. Some do it in order to attract attention to themselves. Others are driven to forgery because they are jealous of the success of other artists or because their own work has not received the attention they feel it deserves. After all, if a painter does not achieve success under his own name but does if he uses someone else's, then it is easy to understand why he resorts to forgery. It is a way of getting his own back on the critics and experts who ignored his work.

Han van Meegeren was perhaps the most famous art forger of them all. He was born in 1889, and started his career as a painter in his native Holland. At the beginning he was fairly successful and all the paintings in his first exhibition were sold. But, after that, the quality of his work deteriorated and, although his pictures were of a high technical standard, they did not win the admiration of either the critics or the public. Van Meegeren decided to take his revenge on the critics who now ridiculed his work. 'I had to teach them a lesson,' he told a visitor later. 'I had to prove, once and for all, their utter incompetence, their shocking lack of knowledge and understanding.' Van Meegeren decided to use forgery as his weapon against the critics. He would paint a picture in the style of the great Dutch master, Vermeer, and dupe the so-called experts.

Van Meegeren set about his task with determination and patience. Before he could start to paint the picture itself he had to find the right materials. If the forgery was to convince art experts it was essential that the canvas and paint he used should be as authentic as possible. Modern pigments and new canvas would easily be detected. It took van Meegeren four years to find the pigments that Vermeer himself would have used. Some of them were obscure: Vermeer obtained his characteristic blue colour from the semi-precious stone lapis lazuli and so van Meegeren did the same. These pigments all had to be ground to a powder by hand so that the particles would look irregular when examined under a microscope. Finding a canvas was an easier matter. Van Meegeren simply bought genuine old ones and either cleaned them or painted over the original pictures. He also prepared special brushes which would reproduce the smooth texture of Vermeer's brush strokes. The main difficulty was that of giving the finished picture an appearance of great age. After many experiments, van Meegeren found that a resin using oil of lilacs provided the most convincing effect.

Van Meegeren ensured secrecy for his experiments by leaving Holland and buying a villa in the south of France. Even his wife did not know what he was doing in his locked studio or why he needed to have a constant supply of lilacs! It was then that he built an oven with electric elements in which to bake the finished picture, and discovered by trial and error the exact temperature and time needed to harden the paint without damaging the canvas.

The preparations were complete. All that was needed now was the picture itself. It took van Meegeren seven months to paint 'The Disciples at Emmaus', his first and greatest forgery. By now he had become so obsessed by Vermeer that it seemed as though the great artist himself was really painting the picture. 'It was the most thrilling, the most inspiring experience of my whole life!' van Meegeren said later. 'I was positive that good old Vermeer would be satisfied with my job. He was keeping me company, you know. He was always with me during that whole period. I sensed his presence; he encouraged me. He liked what I was doing. Yes, he really did!'

When the picture was finished, van Meegeren proceeded with the rest of the ageing process. A coat of varnish was applied to the painting and then he faced the problem of applying the thousands of little cracks which can be seen on any old canvas. Van Meege-

A Newly Discovered Vermeer:

A Work by the Master of Delft Found in a Paris Art Sale and Purchased by a Rotterdam Museum

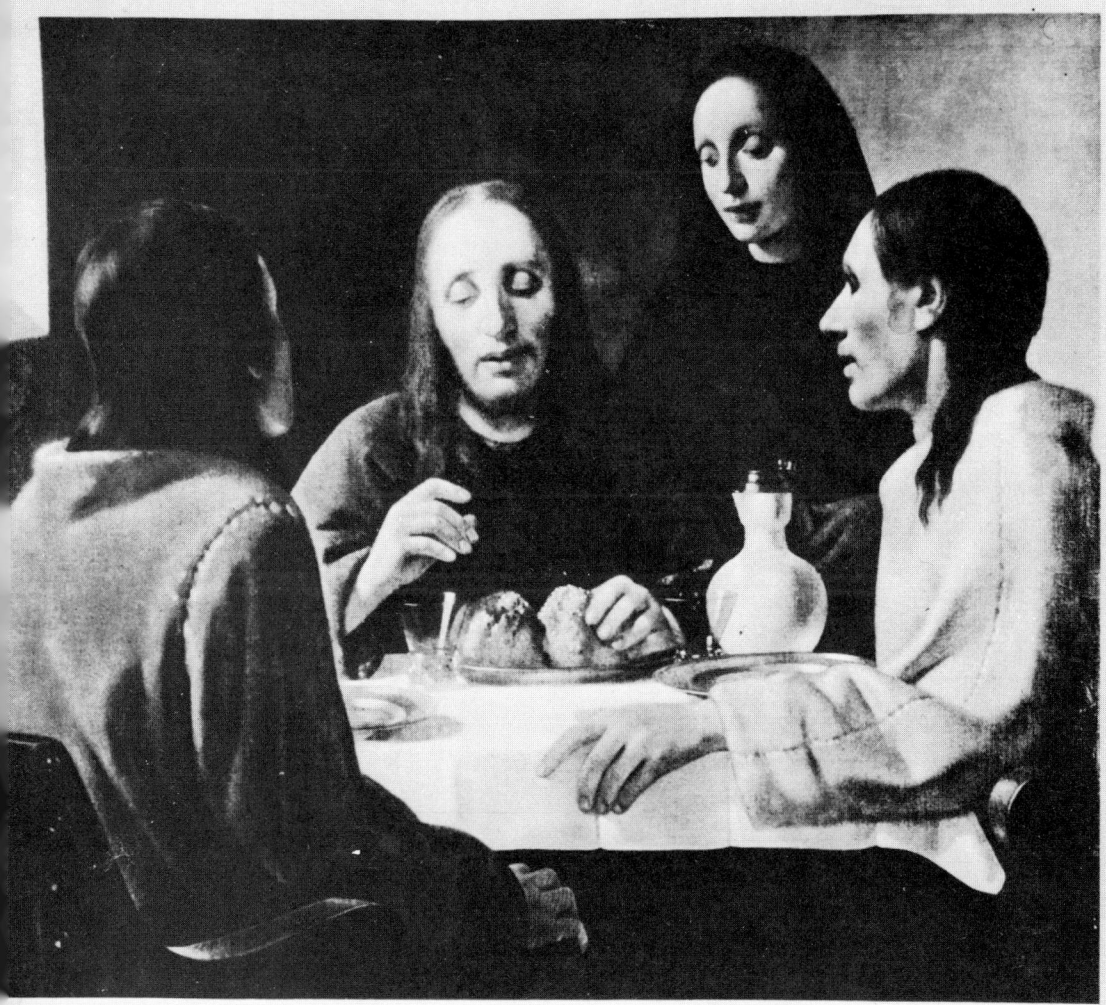

"SHE SAT AT MEAT WITH THEM, HE TOOK BREAD AND BLESSED IT, AND BRAKE, AND GAVE TO THEM, AND THEIR EYES WERE OPENED AND THEY KNEW HIM": It was this supreme moment at Emmaus, when the disciples recognised Jesus following his resurrection, that Vermeer recorded in this hitherto unidentified picture. It came on to the market a short while ago in Paris and, after being recognised as authentic, was purchased by the Boymans Museum at Rotterdam. From the point of view of psychological penetration, depicting as it does a moment of exhaltation, it exceeds any of Vermeer's known paintings

Modern scholarship only recognises forty-one pictures from the hand of Vermeer, but with the discovery of this new masterpiece in Paris yet another work is added, and many will deem it among the finest of this Dutch master's achievements, for it combines at once simplicity, depth, a sense of the dramatic, and a dynamic virility not to be found in most of his works which stand aloof from the world's surging emotions. When the picture appeared in a Paris sale last year Dr. Bredius, an eminent authority on seventeenth-century Dutch art, immediately identified it as a Vermeer, recognising the familiar blue and yellow tones, the master's favourite colours, and the highly individual technique. Thereafter the picture passed into the hands of Messrs. Hoogendijk, art dealers, of Amsterdam, from whom it has been purchased by the Boymans Museum at Rotterdam where it is to be exhibited in the coming summer. The photographs reproduced herewith are the first to be taken

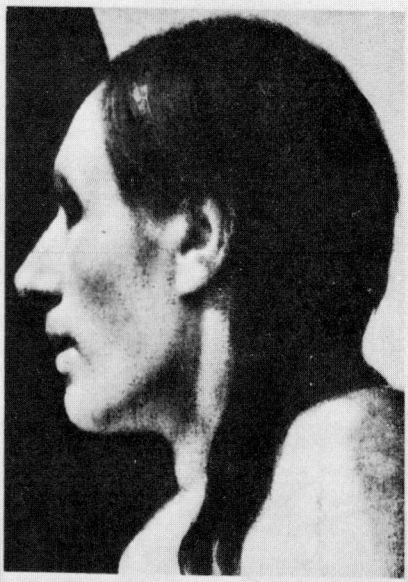

"MONA LISA" VEIN: The face of the woman servant, seen here in detail, is a remarkable piece of characterisation in the newly discovered work by Vermeer, of which nothing was known until it made its appearance in Paris last year

THE RECOGNITION: A detail of the face of one of the disciples from the newly found Vermeer picture. His look of dawning astonishment at the re appearance of the Saviour is shown with masterly skill, conveying a message deeply inspiring

ren solved this by rolling the picture round a cylinder and then filling the resulting cracks with black ink to give the appearance of the accumulated dust of three centuries. It was only when he was quite sure that the picture would stand up under detailed scientific investigation that he set about the task of selling it.

Van Meegeren announced that the picture had come from a Dutch family who wanted to sell it but who wished to remain anonymous for personal reasons. It was inspected by a prominent art expert who was totally convinced by the painting and gave it a certificate of authenticity. The expert, Dr Bredius, announced the great discovery in the *Burlington Magazine* in 1937. 'It is a wonderful moment in the life of a lover of art,' he wrote, 'when he finds himself suddenly confronted with a hitherto unknown painting by a great master, untouched, on the original canvas and without any restoration, just as it left the painter's studio! ... We have here a – I am inclined to say *the* – masterpiece of Johannes Vermeer of Delft.' Other experts rushed to admire the painting, and it was bought by the Boymans Museum in Rotterdam for about £52,000.

Van Meegeren's plan had succeeded. He had painted a picture that was acclaimed by the critics, and the public were flocking to see it. This was the point at which he had planned to reveal the truth. After all, he had achieved what he had set out to do. But the money he had earned prompted him to keep silent and work for more. In the years that followed he painted five more spurious Vermeers, all of which sold for fantastic sums.

By this time the Second World War had begun and Holland was occupied by the Germans. It was now that van Meegeren made a fatal mistake. One of his forgeries, 'The Woman Taken in Adultery', was bought by the Nazi leader Hermann Goering for the extraordinary sum of £165,000. After the war, Allied investigators discovered the picture in Goering's private collection. It had been forbidden for Dutch works of art to leave the country. How, then, did Goering come to possess a priceless Vermeer? The trail led straight back to van Meegeren. He was accused of collaborating with the enemy by selling the picture, and he was arrested as a traitor in July 1945.

Van Meegeren at once confessed that the picture was a fake. After all, the penalty for treason was far more drastic than the

The Master Forger

punishment for forgery. But he had done his work too well. No one would believe that the paintings had been forged. All the experts had acknowledged the pictures to be genuine – it was impossible for them to be wrong and it was preposterous for an accused collaborator to claim that he had painted masterpieces by Vermeer.

The authorities suggested a unique solution to the problem. Van Meegeren must paint a copy of 'The Woman Taken in Adultery'. Van Meegeren refused. He was not a mere copyist – he was a creative artist. He would paint an entirely new Vermeer in front of witnesses, the subject to be set by the court. The authorities agreed and van Meegeren then proceeded to paint 'Christ Teaching in the Temple'. It was not one of his better forgeries but it convinced the court that he could have produced the other paintings.

A commission of experts was appointed to see whether 'The Disciples at Emmaus' and the other pictures were forged or not.

Van Meegeren at his trial

Forgers

Van Meegeren's work had been so skilful that even ultra-violet and infra-red photography revealed no startling evidence. The pictures stood up well to the chemical tests too. All the pigments were found to be authentic – except one. Van Meegeren had slipped up badly when he painted 'The Woman Taken in Adultery' by using cobalt blue for the colour of Christ's robe. This pigment had been used for the first time in the nineteenth century and could not possibly have been known by Vermeer.

In the face of this evidence, the charge against Han van Meegeren was changed from treason to forgery. The trial lasted one day and he was sentenced to one year's imprisonment. But van Meegeren did not live to serve his sentence: he died of heart failure before he could be sent to prison.

Han van Meegeren had won the public attention and acclaim that he had so desperately wanted. His paintings had at last been recognized as masterpieces. It is strange to think that if Vermeer had indeed painted 'The Disciples at Emmaus' it would have been acknowledged as one of his greatest works. And it is strange to think, too, that Han van Meegeren was probably the only forger ever to be asked by a court of law to prove not his innocence but his guilt.

An unclipped coin compared with two clipped coins

13 · 'King' David and the Yorkshire Coiners

The great stretch of moorland which separates Lancashire and Yorkshire is bleak and remote even today. In 1766, when David Hartley brought his wife and family to live there, the moors were even more desolate than they are now. Bell House farm lay miles from the nearest village, and life must have been lonely for the Hartleys, who had moved there from the bustling city of Birmingham.

David Hartley was a skilled ironworker. Why, then, did he come to the bleak West Riding to live on an isolated farm? The answer is simple. Hartley had been in danger of arrest in Birmingham for clipping and coining, an offence punishable by death. By coming to the moorland farm he had hoped to escape arrest and also continue his counterfeiting activities.

Forgers

Coining was a common crime in the eighteenth century. The process was straightforward enough. Gold and silver coins were carefully trimmed or clipped and, after the edges had been remilled, were returned into circulation. The clippings were then melted down and made into new coins with home-made dies and moulds. Although the penalty for this crime was death, poverty and desperation forced many to attempt it. Even respectable people tried their hands at coining, among them the Reverend Edmund Robinson of Halifax, who turned his cellar into a miniature mint, and Joseph Hanson, the Deputy Constable of Halifax, who escaped after his arrest and was never heard of again.

Coin maker's tools

The West Riding of Yorkshire was a popular centre for coiners. The remote farmhouses on the moors were ideal places in which to carry out their operations. The few policemen who existed at that time were based in the towns but, if they did decide to visit a farm like Bell House, their approach would be easily seen and all the evidence hidden before they arrived. David Hartley felt particularly safe from the law – the nearest police were six miles away in Halifax.

Hartley was a ruthless and ambitious man, and he and his two brothers organized an efficient coining operation. He soon became known throughout the district as 'King' David, and his

'King' David and the Yorkshire Coiners

brothers were nicknamed 'The Duke of York' and 'The Duke of Edinburgh'. They and their accomplices clipped as many as a hundred guineas a day, the coins being extorted by force from local people who, in return, were given the coins back together with half the clipped metal.

'King' David became notorious but, although businessmen in the cities clamoured for his conviction, little could be done to stop his activities. The only way in which he and other coiners could be caught was on the evidence of informers, but all attempts to bring him to justice in this way failed. David Hartley's criminal kingdom seemed secure. But not for long.

'King' David's downfall began when the Supervisor of Excise in Halifax decided that his activities should be ended for good and all. William Deighton's job was to supervise the collection of taxes in the area. He found that many honest people were trying to pay their taxes with coins that had been clipped or forged and, as he couldn't accept such illegal payment, his task was being severely hindered by the coiners. Deighton became friendly with an unimportant member of 'King' David's gang called James Broadbent, who agreed to help him to bring the coiners to justice.

Hartley had never trusted Broadbent and, as things turned out, this was just as well, for the informer helped Deighton to trap several minor coiners. The arrests alarmed 'King' David but he did not suspect that Broadbent was to blame.

Deighton was not satisfied with the conviction of minor coiners; he wanted nothing less than the capture of the 'King' himself. He persuaded Broadbent to make a sworn statement implicating Hartley and then he secured a magistrate's warrant for his arrest. Broadbent was to be paid one hundred guineas for his services.

On 14 October 1769, Deighton and two of his bailiffs entered the Old Cock Inn in Halifax. 'King' David had been drinking there with friends for two hours, and his mood was genial and confident. He was astonished, therefore, when Deighton came in, dragged him to his feet, and snapped irons on his wrists. Hartley looked round at his friends for help but they had all slipped away. They knew that there was nothing to be gained by trying to rescue him. Hartley was imprisoned in the tiny Halifax gaol and taken to York the following day to await trial at the next assizes.

It was then that Deighton made the mistake of refusing to pay Broadbent the hundred guineas he had promised him. Broadbent went straight to 'King' David's brother, Isaac, and told him that he had been blackmailed into naming Hartley. He was now prepared to testify that the 'King' was innocent. But the magistrate refused to believe this new story and Hartley was kept in gaol.

'King' David's arrest alarmed and angered the coiners. They were all at risk now and there seemed only one solution to the problem. Deighton must be murdered. Isaac Hartley, 'the Duke of York', now took charge and called a meeting of the principal coiners. They decided that Deighton's death was the only possible revenge for 'King' David's capture. None of them wished to do the deed themselves so it was agreed that someone else should be paid to do it. Isaac consulted his brother in gaol and then announced that he would supply the weapons if the other coiners contributed to a fund to pay the murderers. In the end, two violent criminals, Matthew Normington and Robert Thomas, agreed to commit the murder for a fee of one hundred pounds.

On 4 November 1769, William Deighton left a meeting with friends and set off for home, little realizing that Normington and Thomas were waiting for him behind a wall near his house. As Deighton opened his front gate, the two men raised their guns and pulled the triggers. Thomas's gun failed to fire, but the slugs from Normington's gun reached their mark. Deighton fell to the ground with a wound in his head. Thomas jumped over the wall and hit Deighton viciously with the butt of his gun before helping Normington to empty the dead man's pockets. Then they made their escape.

The death of Deighton had quite the opposite effect to that which the coiners had expected. Instead of removing the threat of arrest, the murder only increased it. Horrified by the events in Halifax, the government imposed harsher penalties for the people connected with coining, increased rewards for informers, and announced their determination to stamp out coining at all costs. The coiners retreated in the face of this opposition. The practice continued but no longer did the coiners have it all their own way in the West Riding, and local people were no longer intimidated by gangs like that of 'King' David.

A full and true Account

Of a barbarous, bloody, and inhuman

MURDER

Committed on the Body of Mr. Dighton, Officer of Excise for the Town of Halifax, on Thursday the 9th Day of November, 1769,

Robert Thomas, Matthew Norminton, and William Fowles, are taken up, thro' the information of James Broadbent, to be the Persons who committed the above murder.

THE above Mr. Dighton had been transacting business all the day of the 9th of November untill the evening, when he chanced to be engaged in company pretty late that night; and as near as can be computed it was eleven o'clock before the company broke up; Mr. Dighton took leave and bid good night, and went by himself towards home, to a place called Bull-Close, about a quarter of a mile from Halifax; he had not got above half way, when he was fired upon by some person or persons unknown; they no sooner saw that he fell down, but, it is supposed, they rushed upon him and stamped on his breast untill he was quite dead, as a person declared who helped to lay him out, that the marks was visible upon his breast of the nails of their shoes; he was seen to have between nine and ten guineas in his pockets, which these villains, after they had committed this horrid crime, took from him. It is thought they watched him so narrowly the same evening, that they knew the house he was engaged in, and the exact time the company broke up; it is likewise thought, that the place where he was shot, the muzzle of the piece was not three yards from him; upon viewing the place where he was shot, it is supposed they concealed themselves in a corner of the field near a gate that led into the lane where Mr Dighton was to pass in his way home, and upon this gate they levelled their piece, as the marks of the flash are to be seen upon both staves of the gate.

Great numbers of people flock daily to the place where he was shot, who are all astonished at the barbarity of mankind, and especially in the unfortunate Mr. Dighton, who had surprizingly industrious in finding out and taking up part of a gang of villains, who are connected together in bodies, in different parts of the country, and carry on their illicit trade of clipping and coining the current coin of of this kingdom. Pity it is that this gentleman should be so suddenly cut off; he had struck such a terror amongst them, that they resolved to kill him, thinking to reign unmolested; but we hope his place will soon be supply'd, and a sharp look out after the offenders, who, we make no doubt will soon be took, and meet with a punishment adequate to their reward.

We have just received the following account concerning the murder of Mr Dighton, thro' the information of one James Broadbent, of Mythomroyd Bridge, near Halifax, who has been in custody some time, and declares the abovesaid Robert Thomas to be the person who murdered Mr. Dighton; proper persons were immediately dispatched who took him in his house at Wadfworth Banks, near Hepton Bridge, and conveyed to Halifax; they likewise brought a pair of shoes, with the heels full of large nails; it is supposed after he was shot, he was stamped upon, as the marks were visible upon his breast.

The above Robert Thomas has a wife and four children in a very poor and distressed condition, but since the murder of Mr. Dighton, he has a load of meal, a large quantity of beef, malt, &c, &c. which it is supposed he bought with the money he robbed Mr. Dighton of after he was murdered.

This day, (the 19th) two more persons were taken up on suspicion of being concerned in the above murder, more are hourly expected.

After the examination of James Broadbent, the Jury summed up the Evidence, and gave it as their Opinion, that Robert Thomas, Matthew Norminton, and William Fowles, were either the Persons, Abettors, or Assistancers, in the Murder of Mr. William Dighton, Gentleman, whereupon the Coroner committed them all to York Castle, to take their Trials this next Assize.

Many arrests were made following the murder. James Broadbent was the first to be taken into custody and it was he who told the police that Normington and Thomas had committed the crime. All three were sent to join 'King' David in the gaol at York Castle.

David Hartley was brought to trial on 2 April 1770. The principal witness for the prosecution was Broadbent, who was then set free as a reward for turning King's evidence. Hartley himself was sentenced to death. On 1 May 1770, the *Leeds Mercury* published a brief report of his execution:

> On Saturday, 28 April, about half-past two in the afternoon, David Hartley, commonly called King David, and James Oldfield, under the sentence of death for coining and diminishing Gold Coin, were executed at Tyburn, near York. At the fatal tree they behaved every way suitable to their unhappy circumstances, though we do not hear that they said anything by way of confession. The report of their having had a reprieve was not true, the Judge having left a discretionary power with the High Sheriff to put off the execution.

Hartley's wife obtained permission for his body to be returned home for burial, and the local people, who had feared and despised 'King' David in life, lined the streets to mourn him in death. He was buried in the churchyard at Heptonstall, the only inscription on his simple grave being: *D.H. 1770*. The church register is more informative: '1770 May 1st. David Hartley of Bell House in the township of Erringden, hanged by the neck near York for unlawfully stamping and clipping public coin.'

Matthew Normington and Robert Thomas were then brought to trial but the evidence against them was thin. No one had seen the murder and no one had even seen the two men in Halifax on the night of the crime. They were acquitted for lack of evidence.

The authorities were determined to find Deighton's murderers and so the search went on. A man named Thomas Clayton was then arrrested for coining and, understandably anxious to avoid the death penalty, told the police that he had seen Normington and Thomas commit the murder. The two men were arrested again and brought to trial. Faced with overwhelming new evidence, they confessed. Normington wrote:

> David Hartley gave me a Sum of Money to shoot Mr Deighton. He, and his Brother Isaac, were the Persons who prevailed upon me to commit the Murder; and David Hartley promised me the sum should be made up to One Hundred Pounds. We attempted more than once to dispatch him, before the Night on which the deed was done; and Isaac Hartley furnished me with the very Piece that shot him ...

'King' David and the Yorkshire Coiners

Upon the word of a dying Man, I protest that no other persons were concerned actually in committing the Murder, but Robert Thomas and myself, nor is it in my power to make any Discovery relative to the Persons concerned in clipping, Coining, &c.

After the execution, the bodies of Normington and Thomas were hung in chains from a gibbet near Halifax, in the hope that 'such a notorious and public example may happily deter any future crimes of so shocking a nature being perpetrated in a neighbourhood that has long been infested with a most dangerous set of villains'.

The reign of 'King' David and his fellow coiners was ended. Their activities prompted the government to establish a fixed weight and size for all coins so that clipping could no longer be a profitable occupation for criminals. The West Riding soon lost its reputation for being 'Coiners' Country' as the criminals were either arrested or else ceased their operations. 'King' David's brother, Isaac, was never caught. He lived on until 1815 and now lies buried in Heptonstall churchyard next to the plain grave of his brother, the King of the Yorkshire coiners.

14 · The Greatest Forgery of All

One morning in May 1945, a few days after the end of the Second World War, villagers living near the Traunsee lake in Austria woke up to an astonishing sight. The edge of the lake was covered with banknotes! When they went to investigate, they found that the money was British currency, thousands and thousands of five, ten and twenty pound notes. The villagers had no idea how the money came to be there. All they could be sure of was that a fortune was lying on the ground, waiting to be picked up. They needed no second invitation. They eagerly collected the damp notes, cleaned and dried them, and returned to collect more. The money had been washed into the lake by the fast-flowing River Traun and, in the days that followed, more pound notes drifted ashore to be collected by the bewildered villagers. An enterprising local fisherman even sailed out into the lake to gather notes in his nets before they reached land.

It wasn't long before news of the astonishing discovery reached the American military authorities who had recently liberated the area from the Germans. They immediately took charge of the money, and began to investigate where it had come from. Soon an even greater discovery was made. Packing cases in an abandoned lorry were found to contain several million pounds worth of British banknotes. But these weren't ordinary notes: they were all brilliant forgeries.

A leading American forgery expert at once set to work to solve the mystery. His search led him to a concentration camp at Ebensee where he found a group of prisoners who had forged the notes. They told him that they had produced counterfeit British banknotes to the value of one hundred and fifty million pounds!

The story of the greatest forgery of them all began at the beginning of the war. The German authorities decided that the production of forged currency would be a good way of under-

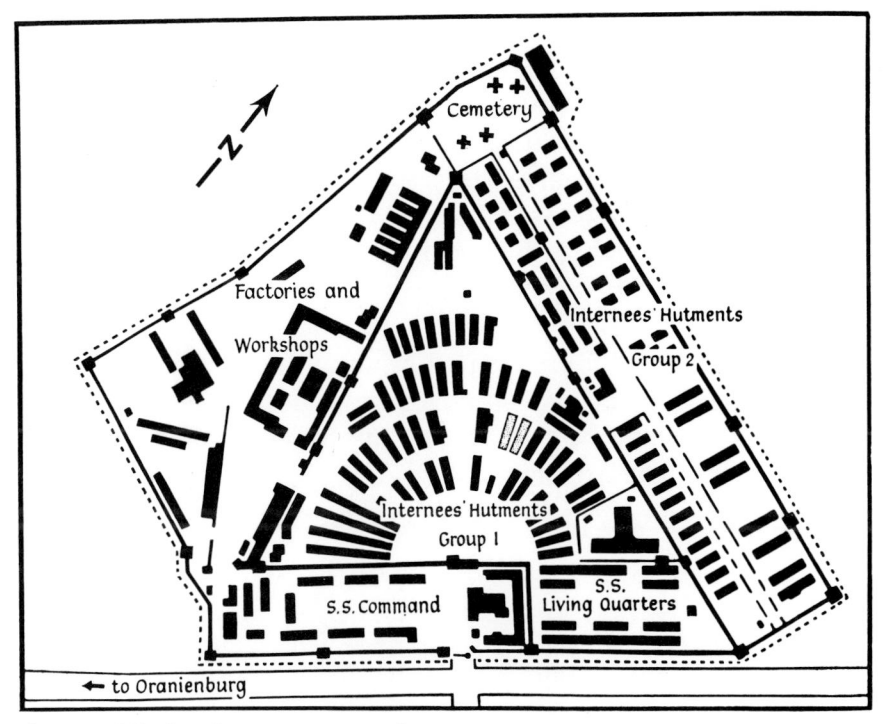

A map of Sachsenhausen concentration camp

mining the British economy and a convenient way, too, of paying their spies and collaborators in neutral and occupied countries. Major Bernhard Krüger was placed in charge of Operation Bernhard, as it was called. He was the head of the workshop which produced the forged passports and documents needed by German agents, and he was therefore the obvious person to organize the forging of British banknotes.

In great secrecy, Krüger gathered together a large team of workers in the Sachsenhausen concentration camp. They were all prisoners but had been selected for their special skills at printing and engraving currency. They lived quite apart from the other inmates and enjoyed special privileges – their quarters were comfortable and their food was of a better quality than that given to ordinary prisoners. They were told that they would have nothing to fear if they worked hard and well.

And so the work began. There were difficulties at first. The engravers found it hard to reproduce the figure of Britannia on the five pound note, and it was some time before they were able to

Forgers

produce paper that would defy detection under ultra-violet light. But these initial problems were eventually overcome and full scale production of the forged notes began.

When they had been printed, the notes were carefully examined in a special inspection section and their quality was assessed. The best notes were to be used only by German agents in enemy countries and for business in neutral countries. Second-class notes were to be used to pay collaborators in occupied countries and for black market operations. The lowest quality notes were reserved for paying unimportant people. The famous spy Cicero was paid three hundred thousand pounds in forged Operation Bernhard notes for the secrets he stole from the British Ambassador's safe in Ankara.

Bernhard Krüger

The forged notes proved so useful to the German war effort that they demanded that production be stepped up. Krüger increased his team of forgers to one hundred and forty men, all organized into specific departments like any other business operation. Their output was now four hundred thousand notes each month, all of which could only be detected as false by experts. Particular attention was paid to detail. At first, the notes were given a worn appearance by chemical treatment. But this proved unsatisfactory and a more time consuming method was adopted. Fifty of the forgers were lined up in two columns and the notes were passed from hand to hand, gathering dirt and perspiration as they went. They were rubbed and folded to give the appearance of continual use. Some of the notes were pierced with a pointed wire, others were scribbled on with genuine British ink. And, as a final touch, they copied a bank teller's habit of writing the total value of a bundle of notes on the top one. This process made the newly printed notes look as though they had been in circulation for years.

Production continued throughout the war but, as the Allies advanced into Europe and German defeat became inevitable, the morale of the forgers weakened. Their skills had kept them alive during the war but they knew that their knowledge of the crime was now a threat to the German authorities. The operation was disbanded and the men were transferred to the camp at Ebensee where they were liberated by the Allies before any harm could come to them.

The undistributed banknotes were removed, too, and so was all the printing machinery. Many of the notes were dumped into the River Traun, where they were later to astonish the people of the Traunsee. Others were found in the abandoned lorry. But the rest found a deeper and more secure resting place.

Toplitzsee is an isolated lake in the Austrian mountains, so remote and unfrequented that no path led to it. It was in the waters of this lake that cases containing Bernhard banknotes and printing plates were sunk during the last desperate days of the war. When the hostilities ended, Allied investigators heard reports that the lake held the secret of Operation Bernhard. A team of British divers was sent to explore the lake but they reported that there was nothing to be found in the dark water. A larger and better equipped American expedition followed but they found nothing either. The bottom of the lake was clogged by a mass of tree trunks, branches and wood. Could the chests be lying beneath this? They tried to blast a way through with explosives but, by the time the divers reached the bottom, the breach had closed again.

Forgers

It was not until 1959 that a final attempt was made to recover the treasure of Toplitzsee – if, in fact, it existed at all. Sophisticated salvage equipment was used, including metal detectors and an underwater television camera. It was now that the lake revealed its secret at last. The television camera was lowered beneath the surface, past the obstruction of branches and trees, until it reached the bottom. And there, covered with mud, lay a case. A grapple hook was lowered and the case was dragged towards the surface. Then, suddenly, it split open, spilling thousands of notes into the water. The camera descended again and another chest was found. This time nothing went wrong. The chest was brought ashore and opened. It contained thousands of forged banknotes, still in good condition.

The remaining cases were brought to the surface. These contained not only banknotes but also printing plates and the Operation Bernhard account books which revealed the full extent of the forgery. And the lake revealed another sunken secret: the records of the German Secret Service.

The story of Operation Bernhard was over, and the greatest forgery of all time had come to an end. But forged Bernhard notes still surface from time to time in Europe, and they are much prized by collectors. Even today, the skill of the forgers of Sachsenhausen can still fool the experts.

15 · The Hungarian Circle

Operation Bernhard was the greatest forgery of all time. The greatest *fraud* of all time was carried out by the Hungarian Circle between 1962 and 1976. Forgery played a vital part in this daring operation which, according to police estimates, defrauded banks all over Europe and the Middle East of at least two hundred million pounds. If the members of the Circle had not been caught in time, their activities might well have wrecked the entire banking system of the Western world.

The plot was uncovered quite by accident. Early in 1976, Scotland Yard became curious about a sudden change in the life style of a well-known Soho bookmaker called William Ambrose, known as Billy the Boxer. Ambrose had exchanged his modest home in the East End of London for a luxury house in the Surrey stockbroker belt and he was now driving a Rolls Royce. The Serious Crimes Squad were suspicious of Ambrose's unexplained prosperity and decided to keep him under constant surveillance. During the next five months he was followed everywhere he went and all the people he met were photographed.

One of the people Ambrose met regularly was a middle-aged man called James Evans. Scotland Yard records revealed that his real name was Henry Oberlander and that he was known to have a criminal record for fraud. Oberlander was followed too, and the police discovered that he made a great many short trips abroad on a variety of faked passports. Each time he returned, Oberlander would bring back with him a bewildering assortment of foreign currencies which he would exchange in London.

It was obvious that Oberlander was up to no good but it was not until police investigated his friends that the truth began to dawn. Oberlander had been born in Czechoslovakia and his associates proved to be of European origin too. Both Emile Fleischman and Andre Biro had been brought up in Hungary and both had

The block of flats where the gang had its headquarters

previous convictions for fraud. But it was only when an Argentinian forger called Francisco Fiocca moved into Biro's Notting Hill flat that the police realized that they had stumbled onto the trail of a major crime. Fiocca was an internationally-known forger who had never been caught; if he was involved with Oberlander and the others then the operation must be a very big one indeed.

The police kept a close watch on all the suspects, disguising themselves as Arab sheikhs, traffic wardens and American tourists in order to keep as close to their quarries as possible. One

The Hungarian Circle

detective was forced to pretend to be a drunken Irishman when one of the gang noticed him outside Biro's flat. His performance was so convincing that a passing tramp asked him for money. The detective gave it to him gladly.

On 13 August, the police raided the flat, and Oberlander and the others were arrested. It was then that Scotland Yard realized that the crime was even bigger than they had at first suspected. The flat was a forgers' den. It contained printing presses, cases of type, machines for embossing gold leaf on documents, stolen passports, visas, stolen airline tickets, forged identity papers and official rubber stamps stolen from foreign embassies. The police also found forged banker's drafts valued at over five million pounds.

As investigations continued, Scotland Yard realized that they had uncovered a gigantic banking fraud and that the gang – known as the Hungarian Circle because of their eastern European origins – had swindled at least two hundred million pounds from banks over a period of fifteen years. One might think that Oberlander and his associates must have been master criminals in order to carry out such a daring operation, but the truth was rather different. The crime was only successful because it proved all too easy to persuade banks to part with large sums of money.

The plan was simple. The Hungarian Circle forged banker's drafts which they cashed at banks in different countries. A banker's draft is similar to a cheque but there is one important difference. A draft cannot bounce; it is guaranteed by the bank which issues it, and so another bank will automatically cash it. The only safeguard is an advice note, a copy of the draft which is sent by post to the bank where the draft is to be cashed. All the Hungarian Circle had to do was to forge the draft for themselves, and then forge a matching advice note to send to the bank of their choice. The drafts were easy to forge. The gang would buy genuine bank drafts for small amounts. All they needed to do then was to print copies on their own printing presses and to copy on to these the authorized signature which appeared on the genuine draft. Then they presented the forged drafts in the selected bank and received cash in exchange. By the time the bank discovered that it had been swindled, the man who had cashed the draft would have disappeared. It was all so easy.

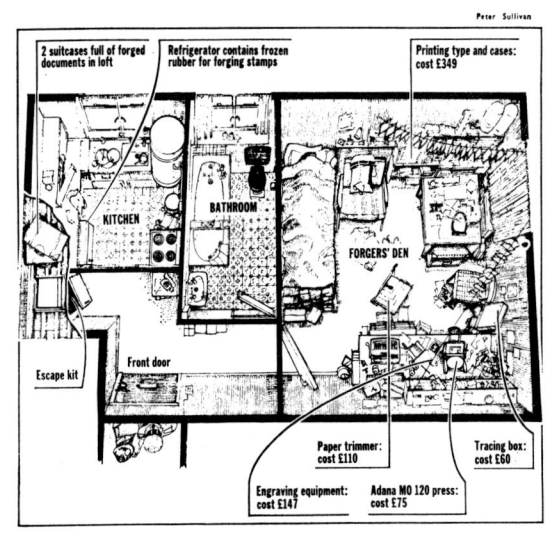

A diagram of the forgers' den

Perhaps the most astonishing aspect of the crime is the fact that the Hungarian Circle managed to get away with it for so long. Many of their drafts were not perfect forgeries: letters in signatures were incorrectly spaced, inks were mismatched, and serial numbers were printed in the wrong type-faces. Some of the gang's identity documents were unconvincing too. And why did the banks not take drastic action to prevent further frauds? They faced a painful dilemma. International banking operations depend on confidence. A leading international bank in London may handle up to six thousand bank drafts a day and they would lose a great deal of business if people knew how easy it was to forge them.

The arrest and conviction of the Hungarian Circle has not ended the story. The police have not been able to recover the two hundred million pounds which the gang made from their operation, and Oberlander and Fleischman have claimed that all the money has found its way into the hands of organized crime in the United States. They have also said that the Hungarian Circle was only a part of a larger organization, and that there are gangs in other countries busy forging bank drafts. Whether this is true or not, it is strange to think that the Hungarian Circle might still be forging banker's drafts in Notting Hill if Billy the Boxer hadn't bought a new Rolls Royce.

16 · Forging Ahead!

The Hungarian Circle and Operation Bernhard were spectacular frauds. Most forgers are less ambitious, and many are never detected. Those cases that are found out often display a degree of imagination and ingenuity that must be the envy of more conventional criminals. Take, for example, just a handful of the forgeries noted during 1978.

In January, two con men earned over five hundred thousand pounds by selling fake bars of gold to businessmen. The gold bars were really blocks of brass which were substituted for the real thing after each deal had been concluded.

A Lebanese syndicate flooded the London gold market with one hundred thousand forged gold sovereigns, acknowledged by experts to be some of the most cunning forgeries ever seen.

Experts at both Christie's and Sotheby's, the distinguished auctioneers, were fooled by forged antique scientific instruments which had really been made in a garden shed in Slough. One of these fakes, a silver astrolabe, was sold by Christie's for five thousand pounds.

A solicitor was jailed for his part in a plot to defraud the Bank of England of more than a million pounds.

It was discovered that hundreds of Greek immigrants were receiving social security payments of up to sixty pounds a week from the Australian government on the basis of forged medical certificates.

A van driver in Leeds forged the signatures of several famous people, including the Queen, Prince Philip, Edward Heath and the entire 1966 England World Cup squad. He then sold them to collectors.

These forgers, and those whose stories I have told in this book, only succeeded because people were willing to believe that a mermaid could exist or that a banknote was genuine. Forgery will

Forgers only die out when human beings cease to be gullible, and when they refuse to be taken in by the forger's art. But there's not much chance of this ever happening. After all, in the words of the great Barnum, 'there's a sucker born every minute!'

Further Reading

Hundreds of books have been written about fakes, frauds and forgeries and it would be impossible to list them all here. The books which follow are those which I found most useful when I was writing this book, and which are most likely to be of interest to anyone who would like to explore the subject further.

ALDINGTON, RICHARD, *Frauds*, Heinemann, 1957.
BARNUM, PHINEAS TAYLOR, *The Life of P. T. Barnum Written by Himself*, Sampson Low, 1855.
COLE, SONIA, *Counterfeit*, John Murray, 1955.
DANCE, PETER, *Animal Fakes and Frauds*, Sampson Low, 1976.
FARRER, J. A., *Literary Forgeries*, Longmans Green, 1907.
KELLY, LINDA, *The Marvellous Boy: the Life and Myth of Thomas Chatterton*, Weidenfeld and Nicolson, 1971.
KLEIN, ALEXANDER, *Grand Deception: the World's Most Spectacular and Successful Hoaxes, Impostures, Ruses and Frauds*, Faber and Faber, 1956.
LARSEN, EGON, *The Deceivers: Lives of the Great Imposters*, John Baker, 1966.
MARSH, JOHN, *Clip a Bright Guinea: the Yorkshire Coiners of the Eighteenth Century*, Robert Hale, 1971.
MILLER, DAVID PRINCE, *The Life of a Showman*, Edward Avery, n.d.
MONTAGU, EWEN, *The Man Who Never Was*, Evans, 1953.
MOSS, NORMAN, *The Pleasures of Deception*, Chatto and Windus, 1977.
PIRIE, ANTHONY, *Operation Bernhard: the Greatest Forgery of All Time*, Cassell, 1961.
POOLE, STANLEY B-R., *Royal Mysteries and Pretenders*, Blandford Press, 1969.
RIETH, ADOLF, *Archaeological Fakes*, Barrie and Jenkins, 1970.
ROSE, JUNE, *The Perfect Gentleman: the Remarkable Life of Dr James Miranda Barry ...*, Hutchinson, 1977.
SANGER, 'LORD' GEORGE, *Seventy Years a Showman*, Dent, 1910.

Forgers

SUMMERS, ANTHONY and MANGOLD, TOM, *The File on the Tsar*, Victor Gollancz, 1978.
THOMPSON, C. J. S., *Mysteries of Sex: Women Who Posed as Men and Men Who Impersonated Women*, Hutchinson, 1938.
WEINER, J. S., *The Piltdown Forgery*, Oxford University Press, 1955.
WERNER, M. R., *Barnum*, Jonathan Cape, 1923.
WHITEHEAD, JOHN, *This Solemn Mockery: the Art of Literary Forgery*, Arlington Books, 1973.

Acknowledgements

The author and publishers would like to thank the following for their kind permission to reproduce copyright material which appears in this book:

Associated Press: p. 45; Professor Blacking: p. 50; Trustees of the British Museum: pp. 55, 57 and 59; Calderdale Library: pp. 73 and 74; Cassells Ltd: pp. 81, 82 and 84; Evans Bros: pp. 41 and 42; Goteburg Natural History Museum: p. 24, right; Greenwich Local History Library: p. 11; Halifax Borough Archive: p. 77; Mansell Collection: pp. 69 and 71; Mary Evans Picture Library: pp. 27, 28, 33, 35 and 61; Radio Times Hulton Picture Library: pp. 12, 18 above, 30 left, 62 and 64; Royal Army Medical College: pp. 36 and 37; Royal Geographical Society: p. 46; The Sunday Times (Peter Sullivan): p. 88; Syndication International: p. 86; Wakefield District Council City Art Gallery: p. 24 left.

The cartoon on p. 48 was taken from *Archaeological Fakes* by A. Reith.

Index

Numbers in italics refer to illustrations

Abominable Snowman, 21
Alexei, Tsarevitch of Russia, 30
Ambrose, William, 85, 88
American Museum, 17–19, *18*
Anastasia, Grand Duchess of Russia, 29–31, *30*
Anderson, Anna, 29–31, *30*
Anderson, Elizabeth Garrett, 38
Animal forgeries, 21–4
Ankara, 82
Archaeological forgeries, 44–54
Art forgeries, 67–72
Australian Magazine, 22

Bank draft forgeries, 87–8
Banknote forgeries, 9, 80–84
Bare-fronted hoodwink, 23
Barnum, Phineas Taylor, 14, *15*, 15–20, 90
Barry, James, 32, 36–8, *37*
Basilisk, 22, *22*
Bedford gaol, 53
Bell House farm, 73–4
Berlin, 29
Billy the Boxer *see* Ambrose, William
Birmingham, 52, 73
Biro, Andre, 85–6
'Bones' *see* Simpson, Edward
Boston, 17
Bosworth, Battle of, 25
Boymans Museum, 70
Bredius, Dr, 70
Bristol, 56–8
British Museum, 44, 47, 51
Broadbent, James, 74, 78
Burgundy, Duchess of, 26, 28
Burlington Magazine, 70

Cape Town, 37–8
Centaur, 21
Chardin, Teilhard de, 44, 48
Charlottesville, 31
Chatterton, Thomas, *55*, 55–60, 61–2, 65, 66
Chelsea Hospital, 34, 36
Chimera, 21
'Christ Teaching in the Temple', 71
Churchill, Winston, 42
'Cicero', 82
Clayton, Thomas, 78
Clipping coinage, 73–9
Cockatrice, 22
Cockney Bill *see* Simpson, Edward
Coining, *73*, 73–9, *74*
Colston's Hospital, 56
Coventry, 35

Daily Advertiser, 17
Davies, Christian, 32–5, *33*
Dawson, Charles, 44–8, *46*
Dawson Dawn Man, 46
Deighton, William, 75–8, *78*
'The Disciples at Emmaus', 68, *69*, 71, 72
Dublin, 32

Ebensee, 80
Edinburgh University, 37
Edward IV, King of England, 26
Edward, Earl of Warwick, 25–9
Eisenhower, General Dwight D., 40
Elizabeth I, Queen of England, 62–3
Erringden, 78

Fairs, 10–14

Index

Feejee Mermaid, *19*, 19–20
Fiocca, Francisco, 86
Fleischman, Emile, 85–8
Flint Jack *see* Simpson, Edward
Fossil Willy *see* Simpson, Edward
Freaks, 10–13, *12*
Fur-bearing Trout, 24

Genoa, 35
Geological Society, 45
Geologists' Association, 49–51, 53
George IV, King of Great Britain, 36
Goering, Hermann, 70
Gomez, Madame, 12
Göteborg Museum, 24
Gray, Thomas, 58
Griffin, 21, *21*
Gruck, 23

Halifax, 74, 75, 77
Hanson, Joseph, 74
Hartley, David, 73–9
Hartley, Isaac, 74–5, 76
Hastings Museum, 48
Hathaway, Anne, 63
Heath, Edward, 89
Henry VII, King of England, 25–9
Heptonstall, 78, 79
Heth, Joice, 15–17
Holborn, 55, 59
Holy Loch, 41
Huelva, 39, 40
Hungarian Circle, 9, 85–8, 89
Hydra, 21

Impersonators, 25–38
Ireland, Samuel, 61–3, 65
Ireland, William Henry, *61*, 61–5, 66

James IV, King of Scotland, 28
Jenny Haniver, 22–3, *23*

Kensal Green Cemetery, 36
'King David' *see* Hartley, David
Koch, Dr Albert, 23
Krüger, Bernhard, 81, 82, *82*

Leeds, 89
Leeds Mercury, 78

Literary forgeries, 55–6
Liverpool, 52
Loch Ness monster, 21
Louis XVI, King of France, 25

Madame Gomez, 12
Madame Stevens, 10–12, *11*
Manuscript forgeries, 55–66, *62*, *64*
'Man who never was', 39–43
Marlborough, 1st Duke of, 32
'Martin, William', 39–43
Meegeren, Han van, 9, 67–72, *71*
Mermaids, 19–20
Miller, David Prince, 13–14
'Miss Molly Gray', 35
Missing Link, 45
Mountbatten of Burma, 1st Earl, 40

Nero, 25
Newcastle, 52
New York, 15, 16–20
New York Evening Star, 16
Nicholas II, Tsar of Russia, 30, 31
Noctifer, 23, 24, *24*
Normington, Matthew, 76–9
Northampton, 52
Notting Hill, 86, 88

Oakley, Dr Kenneth Page, 47
Oberlander, Henry, 85–8
Old Antiquarian *see* Simpson, Edward
Operation Bernhard, 80–84, 89
Operation Mincemeat, 39–43
Orio Rio, 12
Oxford University, 48

Paddington, 34
Pagham, 9
People's Magazine, 49
Philadelphia, 15
Pig-faced lady *see* Madame Stevens
Piltdown Man, 44–8

Ramillies, Battle of, 34
Richard III, King of England, 25, 26
Robinson, Edmund, 74
'Rowley, Thomas', 56–8, 60
Royal Scottish Museum, 23
Royalty Theatre, 35

95

Forgers

Sachsenhausen concentration camp, *81*, 81–3, 84
Sadler's Wells Theatre, 35
St Mary Redcliffe, 56
St Thomas' Hospital, 37
Sanger, 'Lord' George, 10–12
Scarborough, 52
Scotland Yard, 9, 85, 87
Sea serpents, 21, 23
Second World War, 39–43, 70, 80–84
Seraph, 41–2
Shakespeare, William, 62–5
Sheffield, 52
Sheridan, Richard Brinsley, 65
Shirtless *see* Simpson, Edward
Siddons, Sarah, 65
Simnel, Lambert, 25–7, *27*
Simons, Richard, 26
Simpson, Edward (Flint Jack), 48, 49–54, *50*
Snake Billy *see* Simpson, Edward
Snell, Hannah, 32, *35*, 35–6
Sollas, William Johnson, 48
Stevens, Madame, 10–12, *11*
Stoke-on-Trent, 26
Swallow, 35

Tamee Ahmee, 12
Terentius Maximus, 25

Theatre Royal, Drury Lane, 65
Thomas, Robert, 76–9
Toplitzsee, 83–4
Traunsee, 80, 83
Tschaikowsky, Alexander, 30
Twain, Mark, 37–8
Tyburn, 29

Vermeer, Johannes, 67–72
Vortigern and Rowena, 63–5, *64*

Wakefield City Museum, 23
Walpole, Horace, 57–8
Warbeck, Perkin, 25, *28*, 28–9
Washington, George, 16
Welsh, Richard, 32, 34
Whitby, 51
White Russian Shore-Muddler, 24
Whitley, G. P., 22
The Widow in Masquerade or the Female Warrior, 36
'Woman Taken in Adultery, The', 70–71, 72
Woodward, Dr Arthur Smith, 44, 48
Wordsworth, William, 60
Wyatt, James, 53

York Castle, 77
Yorkshire Coiners, 9